Tales of

Tales OF THE *Big Bend*

by ELTON MILES

Texas A&M University Press
COLLEGE STATION

Copyright © 1976 by Elton Miles
All rights reserved

This book has been printed on acid-free paper. The paper also meets
meets the minimum requirements of the American National Standard for Permanence of Paper for Printed Library Materials, Z39.48-
1984. Binding materials have been chosen for durability.

∞

Library of Congress Cataloging in Publication Data

Miles, Elton, 1917–
    Tales of the Big Bend.

    Bibliography: p.
    Includes index.
    1. Tales, American—Texas—Big Bend region.
2. Legends—Texas—Big Bend region. 2. Big Bend region,
Tex.—History. I. Title.
GR110.T5M54   398.2'09764'932   76-17977
ISBN 0-89096-360-6 (pbk.)

Manufactured in the United States of America
SEVENTH PRINTING, 1999

To
LILLIAN NEALE MILES
my partner
in the Heart of Texas
and the Big Bend

Contents

List of Illustrations

Preface

THE MAIN OBJECT of this collection is to tell some of the best tales of the Big Bend. A few of these tales are from old books, but most have come to me from West Texas friends during my quarter of a century west of the Pecos. Something about that rugged and isolated country is conducive to story-telling, for every mountain and desert flat seems to hold a mystery.

Many myths explain natural features and phenomena of the Big Bend. For example, the mountain west of Alpine, with its two notched peaks, is called Twin Sisters because once twin Indian girls in love with the same young man jealously fought over him and became so ill-tempered that the Great Spirit turned them into this mountain to teach them a lesson. The chapters that follow tell how the devil named Mitre Peak north of Alpine, how the image of Christ in the Ojinaga church causes the infrequent and much-needed rain, and why the Chisos Mountains are thought of as "Ghost Mountains" though their name really means something else. As for the Marfa Lights, there seems to be no end to mythic explanations of this eerie phenomenon.

Other stories purport to recount Big Bend history. The result is different and sometimes contradictory stories about the same events. There are several versions, for instance, of the tales that deal with Indian Emily and Dolores at Fort Davis and also of those about the supposed murders over the ownership of Fort Leaton near Presidio. This variation is not surprising, for when a story takes form the teller may well distort the facts on the grounds that "The truth doesn't do it justice," as my friend the late Truman Etheridge used to say. Such lapses from fact to fancy produce not only a better story but very likely a myth or a legend.

It seems all but impossible, however, to recount tales about Fort Leaton or John Glanton, the scalp hunter, without bringing documented history into the telling. These stories do not quite round themselves out without it. Moreover, putting the legends alongside some of the facts makes it possible to compare the events of the tales with what really happened (or did not happen). One also can observe how a legend goes about taking its various forms in repeated tale telling, for in a recently settled country like the Big Bend the folklorist enjoys the advantage of being able to witness the legend-making process.

These Big Bend stories belong to the domain of folklore, and to increase enjoyment of them occasional comments are made on their place within that domain. When asked why a certain folktale was often repeated among the people, folklorist Mody Boatright replied, "It fills a need." We too can cherish a story the more by giving some thought as to why it seems to fill some human need within ourselves. Perhaps all of us would like to be gifted with mysterious power, such as that of the water witch. Perhaps all of us share the yearning of Coronado's Children, as J. Frank Dobie called them, and hope to discover hidden and sudden riches, like the Lost Haystack Mine.

I owe a debt of thanks to my friends of the Big Bend for their good company and the entertaining yarns they tell. Special thanks are due to Joe Graham, folkorist working out of Sul Ross State University, for his freely offered collection of Marfa Lights stories to supplement my own; Carl Appel, horse rancher in the Glass Mountains, for photographs of the Marfa Lights in action; Ross Burns for his Bobcat Carter investigations; photographers Glenn Burgess, Peter Koch, and W. D.

Smithers, long time amigos; and Barbara Stewart, who gave me the notes and photographs of her mother, the late Helen Adams of Presidio. In the text and in the Notes on Sources I have tried to name the many others who have contributed in one way or another.

The first four chapters in this collection make use of material from my articles in the Publications of the Texas Folklore Society. They all have been augmented and updated.

Tales of the Big Bend

1.
The Devil in the Big Bend

THE devil likes it in the Big Bend. The map of Texas from Del Rio to El Paso shows a Devil's River with a Devil's Lake, a Devil's Backbone, a Devil's Ridge, a Sierra Diablo, a Diablo Plateau, and a Cerro Diablo. About halfway between Del Rio and El Paso, where the Rio Conchos flows out of Mexico into the Rio Grande, the border people tell about the local doings of the devil.

The story begins over 350 years ago, when the padres walked with Spanish adventurers up the Chihuahua Trail to La Junta ("The Junction") bearing their crosses in advance of the mounted soldiers and explorers. The settlement—now Ojinaga, Mexico, and Presidio, Texas—was where the two rivers join in the mountainous desert. When the Spaniards arrived, thousands of agricultural Indians lived there in earthen houses and coaxed their living from the sand by irrigating patches of corn and beans.

An old story says that a *cura*, or pastor, came to a small church in La Junta to administer to the Indians. This priest is commonly identified as Cura Urbán, though sometimes he is called Gómez, Pedro, or Urbano. He was faced with a problem, for his parish was plagued by evil touched off by the devil himself. The dwelling place of His Satanic Eminence, the *cura* learned, was a cave high on the northern cliff of a jagged mountain not five miles south of the building in which he preached. From this cave the devil looked upon the entire valley, up and down the two rivers and across to the Chinati Mountains.

Sometimes the devil delighted in terrorizing the people. Standing at the mouth of his cave he would whirl a gigantic lariat, arch the loop across the dry valley of cactus and greasewood for twenty-five miles to Chinati Peak, and pull the rope tight. Up and down this rope the devil would prance and make faces at the horrified Indians, simple farmers trying to work their land for a meager living. It was even more terrible when he galloped up and down the valley floor, bouncing a great iron ball and smashing everything and everybody in his path. With his fiery breath he withered the crops, stopped the rain, and dried up the rivers.

Worse still, he corrupted the morals of the community. Dressed in black, he crept down the mountain at night to whisper evil into the ears and hearts of Cura Urbán's parishioners. Satan thus caused infidelity in the family, rebellion of children against their parents, and a rash of open murder on the three shores at La Junta.

One evening, when the devil came into La Junta for a frolic, a disobedient young girl stole out of her adobe house near the river, slipped through a field of corn, and joined the dancers at a neighbor's house, where candlelight was shining and guitars were strumming. A spooky atmosphere pervaded the dance, presided over by a stranger in black. The young woman's soul chilled with horror when she saw this man approach, walking not on human legs but strutting on scaly, spurred legs like those of a rooster.

He offered her his arm, and mindless of her family and church, she whirled with him among the dancers. As the candles dripped low toward morning the dance ended, and the horrified guests watched the señorita defiantly leave with her hand upon the arm of her demon lover.

Anxiously the valley people waited for dawn. In tears the girl's parents set out at sunrise to find their daughter. In a dry irrigation ditch, splashed with blood in the dust, lay her mangled body, clawed and scratched from face to foot.

And so Cura Urbán found his parish—terrorized, wallowing in sin, and starving because of ruined crops. His first step was to direct his few loyal parishioners in the sawing out and nailing together of a wooden cross. He dedicated that cross to the task of driving the devil out of La Junta.

Despondent over his nearly empty church, Cura Urbán left his room one day and went for a walk east of town toward the devil's mountain. Strolling in meditation through the straggling greasewood, he tried to think of ways to save his parishioners. When he reached the base of the slope, nothing that would help had come to mind. He looked up the mountain to the deeply notched crest. Along this stony route he knew the devil's cave to be. Telling himself that he needed the exercise, he climbed, pushing on toward the devil's domain.

He walked over the gouging stones and through the lechuguilla, growing like clumps of knife blades, until he was halfway to the base of the crevice. On the brink of a cliff far above the valley floor, he met a stranger dressed in black, who leered at him with dagger-point eyes.

"Where are you going, Cura Urbán?" asked the stranger. "And what are you so sad about?"

Desperate to confide in somebody, the padre said, "I despair because people drink, gamble, philander, steal, and break God's law in every way they can think of. What's worse, the devil himself works in the fields and hearts of La Junta to destroy my efforts to save these poor Indians."

Feigning sympathy, the stranger began to gossip about the incidents of infidelity, murder, and robbery, naming names and giving details. To the padre this talk was curious, for the stranger said things which only Cura Urbán could know, things revealed to him in the privacy of confession.

Suspicious, the padre inquired, "Who are you?" He was startled by the stranger's reply.

"I am the devil. In heaven I was never satisfied with my low rank, so I tried to grab the reins of power from God. I was defeated and bodily thrown out of heaven with my rebellious companions.

"As I fell through the sky towards the earth, I knew I was an exile forever from the heavens, so I tried to think of a place where I would like to live. When the mountains and valleys of the earth came into view, I saw far below a tall and pointed peak, which I named 'La Mitra.' When I landed on top of this peak, I saw that beautiful valley below. I knew I could never be happy there because it would remind me too much of the heaven to which I can never return.

'So I spread my wings and started flying again, heading south. When I found this desolate mountain I made my home in this cave, and here I have lived ever since. My purpose is to corrupt the hearts of men and women and to cause wickedness wherever I can. Every night I go into town and whisper into the ears of your parishioners. I tell them to do wrong and to pay no attention to you, Cura Urbán."

With a leer the devil concluded, "I am succeeding in your town, Cura Urbán, and you are failing."

The padre looked up quickly, and in a burst of fury he went at the devil with flying fists. Taken off guard, the howling devil tried to escape by leaping to his rope stretched between the mountain tops and across the valley. The priest, holding before him the wooden cross his faithful few had made, advanced upon the devil. The white magic worked, the cable broke, and the devil fell screaming to the valley floor. Not yet vanquished, the devil scrambled up the mountain, broke off great chunks from the crags and hurled them at Cura Urbán, who was safe behind the holy cross. As a last resort Satan attacked with his iron ball, bouncing it upon the shaking earth, trying to crush the padre. Somehow Urbán stretched the end of the broken rope from the cave to the valley floor. When he again advanced with his cross, the devil dropped the ball with a howl, scrambled up the rope, and hid himself in his cave.

From the darkness inside the mountain Satan yelled and wailed with alarm and spite. To complete his work, Cura Urbán ran up the mountain and rammed the cross into the ground near the mouth of the cave, so that the devil might be forever sealed away under its spell.

The *cura* trudged back down the incline, but his work was not done. He gathered the faithful few in his parish and warned them, "I have whipped the devil and have driven him into his cave, but we must make sure that he stays there."

Obedient to the directions of their leader, they followed him up the mountain, and on the pinnacle above the cave they erected rock walls without mortar to build a shrine, about ten by fourteen feet, with an entrance opening to the north upon the valley. From the river banks they brought four-inch cottonwood logs for rafters and canes to lay across the rafters as a support for the white earthen roof. After leveling the floor with white limestone flour, they placed the cross against a wall in the shrine, that it might stand forever as a charm to keep the devil in his cave below. The mountain was then named El Cerrito de la Santa Cruz ("The Little Hill of the Holy Cross"), and the cave is known to this day as La Cueva del Diablo. (Near Alpine is the prominent Mitre Peak, or, as the devil called it, La Mitra.)

The padre and his followers had one final task. To make sure that La Junta would be safe from the devil, they built a fence across the valley between the mountain ranges to keep him away.

Peace and religion now reigned at La Junta. The people confessed their sins, gave themselves to Christ, and did penance at the shrine on the mountain. Misconduct almost entirely disappeared, and the people came to church regularly, even though they might have only a long shirt with which to cover themselves in the Lord's house.

The victory of Cura Urbán over the devil was so much appreciated that an annual ritual grew from it. Once a year on the third of May, Holy Cross Day, the cross would be taken from the shrine and brought into the valley to bless the crops on all sides of the two rivers, where the devil had once laid them waste.

While the cross was absent from the mouth of the devil's prison, other measures were taken to see that the Evil One did not escape to resume his terrible habits. A day or two before Holy Cross Day the men and boys gathered brush and fire-wood, then brought the fuel on their backs and on burros to build bonfires along the trail to the cave. When the brush piles were ready, lined from the mouth of the cave down the steep path and across the valley of young crops to the river, the priest went up the trail, making the sign of the cross and sprinkling holy water on the brush piles, consecrating them to their holy magic. On the night before Holy Cross Day the fires were lighted. To strengthen the spell, the people around the cave would fire their guns, beat on tin pans, and yell to frighten the devil so that he would not dare appear above ground. Sometimes the brush would be placed so that the fire took the form of a great burning cross on the slope.

In the town, while the men kept the fires burning, women and young people walked in groups about the street, singing. In their song the phrases *"el diablo"* and *"la Santa Cruz"* could be heard.

On Holy Cross Day itself, a procession of devotees took the cross from the shrine and brought it down the trail to the valley farms, where the priest, followed by the procession, carried the cross about in the fields, blessing the crops and praying for a fruitful yield of cotton, corn, beans, and melons and for plenty of water in the river. At the end of the day the procession filed back up the mountain and restored the cross to the shrine.

This annual celebration seems to be slowly dying out, and there are now three crosses in the chapel instead of only

one. Until recently on each Holy Cross Day the faithful removed the crosses from the chapel at four in the morning and
carried them down the mountain and across the field to the
house of a Señora Samaniego. The crosses were kept there
until May 17 and then restored to the shrine. Fires have not
been lighted on Holy Cross Day in several years, but they
are still sometimes burned on Hallowe'en to forestall a
witches' orgy in the region of La Cueva del Diablo.

What might be the source of the Devil tale? Mody C.
Boatright has said that perhaps the myth and the ritual derive
from the Indian's fear of supernatural influence over human
well-being and his desire to appease that power and also
from the early Spanish missionaries' attempt "to phrase the
message of the Church in terms which the Indian could com-
prehend." As though to confirm Boatright's judgment, the story
points to Spanish missionary activity of two and three hundred years ago when it speaks of naked Indians coming to
worship in long shirts so that they might be decently covered.

The shrine still serves year round as a place of worship,
as in many another Southwestern community with a mountain
shrine nearby. In earlier times penitents used to walk barefoot up the mountain to atone for sin. Several elderly residents
of Ojinaga and Presidio have made sure of their atonement
by walking with bleeding feet across the sharp stones to the
cross to pray for forgiveness. A woman in Alpine proudly says,
"My grandmother is one who left blood on the mountain."
Fifty years ago an observer noticed spots of blood along the
trail as he climbed to the shrine. Today there is no such evidence; instead, worshippers dressed in their Sunday finest
climb the mountain to pray and to enjoy a holiday outing.
When I visited the shrine a family was descending the mountain, having carried a sick child up there to pray for recovery.

The little stone chapel still stands and still shelters a
wooden cross, now neatly covered with green cloth but presumably the same cross used by Cura Urbán to keep the devil
out of La Junta. The cross extends about six feet from floor to

ceiling and is adorned with a white veil and a necklace of paper flowers. It is flanked by two smaller wooden crosses, also draped with veils. All three crosses are decorated with sacrifices and emblems that worshipers have left—mirrors, necklaces, rosaries, paper flowers, and letters scrawled to patron saints. Other letters hang from the rafters, and their dates show that the shrine has been in constant use. Fifty years ago, boxes with burning candles set in bottles were placed before one cross. Candles now burn in tumblers, where they are less likely to be put out by strong mountaintop winds blowing through the entrance. Each devotee once was obligated to bring at least one candle to insure that there would always be candles in the chapel. Nowadays an old broom stands in a corner, so that a visitor may sweep out the orange peels or candy wrappers left by a less tidy predecessor. On the south wall opposite the door, a bench, formed by a six-by-six timber about five feet long laid across two stones, provides a cool and quiet place for rest and meditation.

Though the devil is imprisoned in his cave with its entrance dynamited, he still is seen occasionally in the shape of strangely malformed animals. Once a group of playing children saw a burro without a tail; when they called to their parents to look at the funny burro, the animal disappeared into thin air. Sometimes a jack rabbit is seen dancing on his hind legs, as Satan used to dance on his rope. An old woman, more curious than cautious, observed that this dancing rabbit had no forepaws. When she reached out to take the strange animal, it disappeared, causing her to stick a painful lechuguilla thorn into her hand. At times the devil appears as a sow with the face of a beautiful woman. The siren sow is followed by little pigs, all of which have the same face. In this form especially, the devil falls in behind those who have drunk too much tequilla as they cross a dry river bed. With the sow and her pigs following, the poor drunkard fights, breaks windows, and does evil he would not otherwise do.

At least twice the devil in grotesque human form slipped

through the barriers erected by prayer, burning fires, and charms, once on Holy Cross Day itself. In the form of an impish little hunchback, he joined the procession trailing behind a priest as he moved from field to field blessing the crops. While the priest chanted and the people tried to act sober and devout, the little hunchback created havoc, leading ladies into mud puddles, making the dogs howl, pushing men and boys into the river, and breaking people's garters. It was a mad Holy Cross Day.

On another occasion—and to this day many Big Bend families carry the tradition as an experience of their grandmothers—a group of little girls were playing grownup in the streets of Ojinaga. Dressed in their mothers' old long skirts, they joined hands, danced in a ring, and sang a naughty song about the effects of marijuana. They should have known better, for the utterance of evil words brings on real evil. But they sang of how marijuana makes the smoker lurch and makes him talk funny and makes his eyes wobble in a peculiar way. Suddenly there sprang from the ground in the center of the ring a terrible, toothless old hag in dirty flowing rags of black, her eyes flashing crimson rays upon all about her. The children screamed, scattered, and ran. To this day the red eyes of the black old hag are vividly remembered.

In later years a counter legend developed among skeptics to explain away the devil story. They say that a priest in Ojinaga, before the devil myth developed, knew of a cache of gold hidden in the cavern. Finding two men who seemed trustworthy, the padre sent them up the mountain to bring the gold to him so that it could be spent in building a new church. The men proved unreliable, stole all the treasure they could carry, and skipped across the Rio Grande to the United States. To save what was left of the gold, the priest invented a legend to the effect that the devil lives in the cave and holds under his power that area between the shrine and the mouth of the cave. Thus thieves are discouraged from entering the cave to steal the rest of the gold. As for the devil's ball, another tale claims it once was a prized possession of Malinchi, the mistress and guide of Cortez, the conquistador.

Whatever its origin, the legend of the Devil in the Big Bend persists. It is said that the stone foundations of the international bridge at Presidio were laid one moonless night by the devil himself. Also, an iron ball is on public display at Ojinaga today, in Saragosa Street, its lower side tapered into a shaft buried in the ground. V. J. Smith guesses that it probably is a pestle formerly used at a mine, perhaps at Shafter, to crush ore for a smelter. But if anybody in Ojinaga is asked to explain what it is, he will say, "*El bol del diablo.*" It is supposed to be the same iron ball in the very place it was dropped by Satan as he fled before the cross of Cura Urbán up the rope to the hole in El Cerrito de la Santa Cruz. There the devil patiently lies in wait, looking for a chance to sneak back into the valley and work his evil again.

2.
Christ in the Big Bend

THE story of the Devil in the Big Bend is not the only one that accounts for the chapel with its three crosses on El Cerrito de la Santa Cruz near Ojinaga. Another legend says that in the 1780s a Christian Jumano Indian, Juan Sabeata, saw in the night sky a burning cross hanging over this hill. Taking the vision as a sign, he led a troop of fellow Christian Jumanos on foot up the Rio Grande to the cathedral at El Paso del Norte. There he won the bishop's promise that a priest would be sent to Presidio if he and his brethren would build a duplicate of the grand El Paso church. This the Indians did, the bishop kept his promise, and the little chapel on top of the mountain commemorates Sabeata's fiery vision. The next time Sabeata went to confession, however, he admitted that he was lying, that he never saw a burning cross. The priest may have been exasperated, but they say that Juan Sabeata was happy, for God, moving in his imponderable way, had used his aberration to provide the town with a church.

Connected with that church are stories about its wooden image of Christ, which has jointed neck, arms, and legs. It is said to work miracles.

Called Nuestro Padre Jesús Nazareno, this Cristo hangs in agony on its cross behind the altar. No visitor who sees it will ever forget it. The crown of thorns gashes into the brow. The stiff, disheveled hair bespeaks hours of torment. The half-open mouth is parched, desperate for water. The eyes are rolled to the setting point of death and the hands extend rigidly in utmost pain. Because the high cheek bones suggest Indian features, the carving is said to be of native American workmanship.

An eighteenth-century painting also in the church depicts a priest holding a Cristo in his hand as wide-eyed Indians look on. A lengthy lettered discourse on the canvas, dated July 28, 1798, says that Franciscan Father Pedro Antonio Camargo came there as chaplain about 1790 and left "one of the statues of Jesús Nazareno with hinged joints for three movements" and also a painting of Mary, the "Divina Pastora." The inscription says, "Upon his arrival the Presidio lacked water, asking the Chaplain with all Christians supplicating for relief," but the blessing of rain was withheld "until Jesus arrived." After the rain fell "the barbarians adored Him and a gentile prayed to it also." The commemorative canvas seems to be a contract of sorts, stating clearly that there was "a little chapel built declared for eternal memory so that the image of Patrón Jesús and Patrona Divina Pastora . . . belong to the neighbors and inhabitants of Santiago del Norte" (the early name for Presidio del Norte, later Ojinaga).

Regardless of what the painting says, many tales give different accounts of the origin of the Cristo. Supposedly one day a long time ago a stranger stopped and asked for a night's lodging at an adobe farmhouse in the green valley at the foot of El Cerrito de la Santa Cruz. The woman of the house gave him his supper and showed him to his room.

Next morning the stranger did not appear for breakfast. Having waited beyond her patience, the hostess opened the door a crack and peeked in. To her astonishment the bed had not been slept in, and on the floor was a mysterious box about the size of a coffin. Soon her surprise was overcome by curiosity, and she lifted the lid. With a start she saw lying in the box a life-size image of Christ.

She fell to her knees, crossed herself, then quickly arose, shut the box, threw a black mantilla over her head, and dashed out of the house. She ran along the sandy road into the valley of Ojinaga. Breathless, she entered the cool church, did her obeisance before the altar, and found the priest.

"Padre!" she exclaimed. "Only yesterday a man came to find lodging in my house, I gave him a bed for the night, and today he is gone. Instead there is a beautiful image of Nuestro Padre Jesús in a great box."

The priest marveled at the apparent miracle, put on his black hat, and went with the old woman as she retraced the path to her farmhouse. She showed the priest where the image lay. He crossed himself for protection against black magic and lifted the lid.

To the old woman he said, "Señora, this is a beautiful work of art. A miracle of God brings it for us to place in our poor church at Ojinaga. But it is much too fine a figure for our little run-down church. We must have a larger and nicer building, one that is worthy of this miraculous image."

The priest went to the window and looked south across the desert at the white road twisting its way between dry mountains in Mexico south of the Big Bend. He said, "I must show this statue to the bishop in Chihuahua. I've begged for money to build a new church but he won't listen. If I load this image on a wagon and drive to Chihuahua, perhaps the bishop will be convinced. When he sees the beauty of the statue and hears about the miracle, I am sure he will give us money for a better church."

Before the day was over, the priest was on his way with a mule hitched to his wagon, in which lay the image secured with ropes. As he passed along the road around the base of the cliff where the devil's cave looks out upon the valley, he shuddered and crossed himself. When the wagon had passed halfway around the mountain, the mule stopped.

The padre urged the mule on with the lines. The mule would not move. Was this work of the devil?

"Mule!" he cried. "You are drawing a divine burden. *Arre!* You are doing the work of the Lord!"

Still the mule, baking under the hot sun, balked and refused to comply. The padre whipped the mule, but the wheels stood motionless. He yelled and whipped all at once. Still the mule, though flinching, would not go.

As a last resort the priest drew up his black skirts, climbed down from the wagon, and knelt in the road. He prayed that the mule be suffered to go on down the trail to Chihuahua so that his little town might have a new church. As he prayed the air began to stir. The wind lifted gusts of biting sand before it. Black clouds boiled up in the sky, shafts of lightning speared the ground, and rolling thunder rocked back and forth between the mountains. Rain began to pock the sand, then came down in torrents.

Rainwater pouring from his hat brim, the priest concluded, "The image does not want to go to Chihuahua. It wants to stay here in the place for which it is intended. This image can never be taken from Ojinaga." He climbed back into the wagon, reined the mule around, and drove back through the downpour to his little church. He took the image inside and placed it where it belonged.

Next day when the priest told the people of the valley what had occurred, they decided to do something special to commemorate the miracle. They built a little shrine on top of El Cerrito de la Santa Cruz as a memorial to the miraculous acquisition of the image.

Another tale about the origin of the image is related to the devil's cave story but not to the origin of the shrine. When it is told how the devil was imprisoned, there sometimes follows the story of how shortly afterward a good and handsome man appeared in the town of Ojinaga. Strangely he never grew old, and the people came to accept the eternal youth of the stranger, who lived with them for a hundred years, giving to the poor and encouraging the downhearted.

One day he failed to appear in his usual haunts. The people sought him everywhere, but he was not in the plaza, nor in the church, nor at work in the fields. In the evening as the church bells began to ring, they quit the search and filed along the narrow streets to worship. They entered the church, knelt before the altar, and rased their eyes to behold a miracle.

Behind the altar was a beautiful image of their young stranger. There could be no mistake, he was the same. Marveling, they read at the foot of the image the words, *Nuestro Señor Jesús.*

A continuation of this story is the one that tells of how a beautiful lady appeared in Ojinaga just after the disappearance of the miraculous young man. She also lived in the village a hundred years, helping the needy, winning the love of all, and never growing old. At the end of another century she also disappeared. The people searched and gave up only to answer the evening call to worship. There in the church stood a new statue—an image of their kind lady—and the words at the foot of this one read, *María, Madre de Dios.*

Another account is similar in general outline. It is said that in the days before Ojinaga had a church, an elderly man approached a group of men and women working their fields. He asked them if they wanted to buy his statue, an image of Christ, for their proposed church. The farmers said they would like to see it before they made up their minds. The old man told them to meet him at a certain time and place and they would try to come to terms.

When the people arrived to discuss the transaction, they found a beautiful image of Christ standing where they were to meet the stranger. They waited, but the stranger did not appear. The priest and the people decided that the image was somehow a miraculous gift from God, so they decided to build their church on the spot.

As in the other tales, this priest also thought it best to take the image to Chihuahua to convince the bishop that Ojinaga should have a fine church. The priest loaded the image on a mule, but the mule would not move. Concluding that the load was too heavy for the animal, he placed the image in a wagon and started out. He had gone but a little way when the wheels fell off the hubs and the wagon bed landed flat on the road. Everybody decided that the image did not want to go to Chihuahua. The priest wrote to the bishop to tell him about the divinely stubborn mule, and he sent money for a fine church, which was then built for the image.

A story heard by Ted Sánchez differs in some details. A long time ago, he said, the priest at Ojinaga decided his church desperately needed an image of Christ. As the church could not afford a fine, expensive image, the padre decided to have a cheap one made of clay. He called in two artists to make it. Asking no questions, they apparently set to work, though they were never seen either modeling their image or going about in the town. It was rumored that they worked at night and slept all day.

When the artists had finished their task, they summoned the priest to see whether the image was satisfactory. He complimented them on creating a marvelous work of art and promised to return next day to pay them. When he came back, the artists had mysteriously disappeared. They were never found and never received their pay, but they left behind the beautiful image to comfort and inspire the worshipers in the twin towns of Presidio and Ojinaga.

A tradition arising from these tales about the image of Christ in the Ojinaga church is that God will not allow either the image or its vestments to be taken from the church or from the town. This tradition has its exception, however, in a story that is related in its details to the stories about the origin of the image.

They say that the people of Julimes, a village to the south, once wanted to borrow the figure of Christ to use in a special mass in their small church. Two messengers from Julimes came to Ojinaga to ask the padre for permission to take the image. The padre agreed, and the figure was loaded carefully onto a wagon.

The two men had gone but a few miles when a storm

broke, with much lightning and thunder. Because of it, they were forced to turn back to Ojinaga.

The next day was clear, so the men from Julimes again started out with their miraculous cargo. They had gone only a short distance when the load seemed to grow too heavy for the mules. The drivers urged the animals on, but they would not stir. They grew so tired that they lay down in the road with their harness about them in a hopeless tangle. One of the drivers jog-trotted back to Ojinaga and told the priest what had happened. The priest came out to the scene to judge the problem for himself. He looked at the load and the mules, then knelt upon the ground. He informed the image, "They are taking Thee there for only a short while and will bring Thee back safely." No sooner had he pronounced these words than the mules were on their feet, plodding toward Julimes with the reconciled Cristo.

Irreligious or evil forces may not tamper with Ojinaga's marvelous image. According to a story Carolina Molinar told Ted Sánchez in 1972, it was in the 1790s that the Ojinaga people wanted a Cristo in their church to protect them from the Mescalero Apaches. A couple living near the river found a stranger who volunteered to make the image. All he wanted was plenty of wax and a room to work in alone for a month. He disappeared into the room and was not seen for thirty days. Then the room was opened, and there was the statue. The artist was never seen again.

When the archbishop of Chihuahua saw this Cristo, he became envious and ordered that it be taken to his cathedral. But the crate he had built for it would not go through any of the doors. When the archbishop promised the Cristo he would bring Him back, the crate slid outside with no trouble. By the time the crate had been loaded on a mule-drawn cart and was on its way to Chihuahua, the archbishop had changed his mind. When he did, the back of one of the mules snapped and the cart stopped. (Because of this miracle La Mula, Mexico, got its name.) On his knees the frightened archbishop promised the statue that if He would only let Himself be taken to Chihuahua so that a wax impression could be made, he would bring Him back to where He belonged. Thereafter all went well, because the archbishop kept his word.

In 1973 Russell Gardenier heard it somewhat differently. In the 1860s, when Benito Juarez disenfranchised the Catholic Church, some official decided that Nuestro Padre Jesús Nazareno should be placed in a museum in Chihuahua. In spite of protests from the priest and the people, the government man hired a mule and loaded the statue on it.

The mule lay down and refused to move. Another mule was summoned, with the same result. Five more mules refused to obey the bureaucrat, who then made a speech about what an honor it was for the mule that would agree to bear the Cristo to Chihuahua. The crowd did not know what to do. Then a wrinkled, old peasant limped forward, leading an aged mule named Josefina. The old man said he would take the job and whispered words of conspiracy into Josefina's ear.

Down the Conchos River trail went the little caravan toward Chihuahua. They camped at El Nogal and next day passed through La Macoya and Almo Chapo, still in Nuestro Padre's parish. In the afternoon they came to a small, unnamed settlement of huts around a well about thirty miles south of Ojinaga, near the parish line.

As the group rested and filled water bags, Josefina lay down under a shade tree to rest. When the official told the old man they were ready to push on, he replied; "Josefina is dead." The government man was astounded.

"Beyond this point," said the old mule driver, "the honor was too great for her."

Beaten by the miraculous refusal of the statue to leave the parish, the government man gave up. Another mule took the image back to its rightful place, and La Mula had been named.

In 1912 history again connected with the Cristo. Ojinaga was in the hands of revolutionists. Many fought in patriotism, but a few sought only loot and adventure. As Kate Davis heard it, a troop of Pancho Villa's men forced their way into the Ojinaga church and used it for a barracks. The people complained, and the priests led them in prayer in front of the church. Inside the men cooked the pets and livestock they had taken from the people. They tore down the benches to make beds and threw small images aside to make room to play cards.

In the night they noticed something strange about Nuestro Padre Jesús on His cross. Sweat was running down the face from the crown of thorns. This so frightened the Villistas that they grabbed their things and abandoned the church. The priests then led the people in prayers of thanks.

As Ted Sánchez heard it, the intruders in the church all were hoodlums taking advantage of revolutionary turmoil. Laughing at what they called "superstition," they went hell-raising into the sanctuary and tore the robes from the image of Christ. They meant to take them outside and show them off in the streets as proof of their audacity.

While they were desecrating the church, there was rifle fire from the Federals who were attacking the town. The bandits drew their pistols and ran out into the street. Each was killed as he emerged from the building. The last man, who was carrying the cloak of the Cristo over his arm, was drilled by a bullet just before he made it to the door. He fell dead inside the church—grim proof that nothing pertaining to the image can be carried with evil intent from the church.

Today the image still stands behind its altar in Ojinaga. Reportedly the hair and fingernails grow and have to be trimmed. In time of drought the image goes out at night and walks the fields to bring rain. (The 1798 canvas tells how it broke a drought.) On mornings after a rain, the vestments of the image are wet and muddy, with goathead stickers clinging to the robes. In that dry land Christ seems to serve as rain god and deity of agricultural fertility, while the devil with his fiery breath takes the role of a drought god.

These legends of Christ in the Big Bend attribute power and personality to the image. When the story is told by the Mexican, he does not say it was God's will that the image should remain in Ojinaga. Rather, he says, "The statue did not want to go to Chihuahua."

3.

Chisos Ghosts

STANDING inside the V formed by the Big Bend of the Rio Grande are the mountains known as Los Chisos. They have been called that for almost two hundred years and until recently their name was almost always said to mean "the ghosts."

In 1787 a Spanish Indian fighter of the north Mexican frontier reported, "I have . . . discovered that Zapato Tuerto [an Apache chief] was attacked in the Chisos and not in the Sierra del Carmen." In 1852 the mountains were officially named Los Chisos because that is what they were still called by Mexicans living south of them in Mexico: as part of a United States government surveying party M. W. T. Chandler passed with his pack train south of the Big Bend canyons, and he reported that "this cluster, rather than range of mountains . . . is known as 'Los Chisos.'" If either the old Spanish soldier or Chandler had heard that *chisos* was supposed to mean "ghosts," he did not mention it.

What seems to be the earliest published association of *Chisos* with "ghosts" came forty-seven years later in a report by a second government surveyor, Robert T. Hill. In 1899, with a beaver trapper and a Mexican interpreter, Hill floated and dragged his boats down the Rio Grande from Presidio, through all the Big Bend canyons, to Langtry. Of the mountains which he admired from the river, he wrote: "The crowning feature of this desert is the lofty and peculiar group of peaks known as Los Chisos ('ghosts'). These weird forms are appropriately named. . . . The vertical slopes of the peaks, rifted here and there by joints and seams, give to them the aspect of being clad in filmy drapery. Wherever one climbs out of the low stream groove, these peaks stare him in the face like a group of whiteclad spirits rising from a base of misty gray vegetation." In this account, Dr. Hill was also the first to associate the name *Chisos*, thought to mean "ghosts," with the physical appearance of the mountains.

But he was not the last, for some say that on moonlight nights the white limestone peaks rub shoulders with their igneous companions, like mountainous spirits among the darker crags. (According to geologists, there are no limestone mountains in the Chisos.) Others contend that Los Chisos are so called because of the spooky effect of the moonlight on their gray vegetation. Another reason is that on nights after a rain the mountains glow with phosphorescent light. Patches of light may be seen on a mountain slope, or sometimes an entire peak will glow as though illuminated from within. Bob Clanton of Fort Davis recalls that one night while on a camping and hunting trip he saw an entire valley light up. For an instant, as bright as day, every cactus and rock became distinct.

Another kind of light reportedly moves across the highest peaks and ridges—a ghostly torch carried by the spirit of an Indian warrior stationed in the Chisos to guide other spirits to the Happy Hunting Ground. John Devenport of Alpine heard that the light actually is not an Indian-spirit light at all, but rather a star, seen only in the Chisos, that moves horizontally and counterclockwise. In this analytical day and time the horizontal star is explained away: there are those who say that, with so many stars rising in the clear Big Bend skies, the illusion of a horizontally moving star is created when a newly rising star displaces its neighbor which rose but a moment earlier.

A final "natural phenomenon" explanation of the "ghost"

association with the name Los Chisos supposes that when the first Spanish explorers saw these mountains the peaks were shrouded in mist. Because the vaporous clouds seemed like ghosts, the Spaniards named the mountains "The Ghosts," that is, Los Chisos. Therefore, they say, *los chisos* is a Spanish phrase meaning "the ghosts." It happens, however, that there is no such word in Spanish as *chiso*.

Many know this and proceed to explain the place name Los Chisos as a corruption of the Spanish word *hechizo*, which means "bewitched" in the fearful sense and sometimes "charming" in the complimentary sense. It is the second, rarely used, sense that almost always is appealed to when it is explained that *chisos* is a shortened form of *hechizos* and that *Los Chisos* therefore should be translated as "The Charming Mountains" or "The Delightful Mountains."

Another legend has it that *chisos* is an Apache Indian word for "ghosts" and that the mountains were named by Apaches who made them a hiding place, as they did the Davis Mountains to the north. The late Walter Fulcher of Terlingua, one of the first to seriously investigate the word's meaning, wrote, "I have heard certain clicks, grunts, and sneezes said to be the Apache way of referring to a disembodied spirit. None of them sounded like *chisos*." Confirming Fulcher, Apache language expert Harry Hoijer writes from the University of California at Los Angeles that the word for "ghost" is something like *t-shindee*, adding, "This word is very unlikely as the source of *Chisos*."

To depart from the "ghost" association, it is reported also by Fulcher that *chisos* was said by an old Mexican called El Santo to be the Spanish plural form of an Apache word *chis*, meaning "clash of arms in battle." According to El Santo, at night in the mountains "the clash of steel on steel" could be heard "as the ghosts of Spanish warriors killed in battles with the Indians, came out to fight their battles all over again." But, writes Hoijer, "I know of no Apache word like *chis,* nor any that has the meaning of 'clash of arms in battle.' "

Approaching nearer to what seems the truth about the name of these mountains, an old-time freight wagoner named Tom Burnham, who came to the Big Bend in the 1870s, told Walter Fulcher that Los Chisos were named for a tribe of Indians. Also, a Mexican regarded by Fulcher as quite intelligent and observant "had heard that the mountains got their name from a tribe of Indians, called in their own monosyllabic language *Chis-sah.*"

Further circumstantial evidence indicates that Tom Burnham and Fulcher's Mexican friend probably were right. It is a fact that Los Chisos bear the name of a tribe of Indians, namely, the Chisos, spelled also Chizos. Some ethnological maps place the aboriginal home of the Chisos Indians squarely in the Chisos Mountains and the surrounding Terlingua desert area.

In addition, there is plentiful evidence to suggest that *los chisos* is the Spanish plural form of a widespread Athapascan (Apachean) language-family word which refers to the Apache Indian and means "forest dweller." No dialect of Apache has a plural form for the noun. *Chisos,* except as a name for Indians, is not a Spanish word. Two Lagunero names for the Apache are *chishye* and *tsi-se.* An early Navajo word for the Chiricahua Apache was *chi-shi.* The Apache's name for himself is *shis-inday,* meaning "forest dweller," which they called themselves from their custom of making their winter camps in wooded, mountainous areas. As Harry Hoijer says, "The Lipan word closest to *Chisos* is their tribal name, roughly *chishi.* This might be the source of *Chisos.* . . . *Chishi* is said to mean 'people of the forest.' " The Lipan's region was west of the Pecos River and north of the Rio Grande.

With the absorption of the Chisos Indians into other Apache groups, *los chisos* lost its usefulness except as a place name—the mountains known as Los Chisos in the Big Bend National Park, Chisos Spring east of these mountains, El Vado de los Chisos (Chisos Crossing on the Rio Grande, known in

English as Comanche Crossing), and at least two localities in Mexico south of Ojinaga called Chisos.

Whether or not *chisos* is a Spanish pluralization of the Apache word for "forest dweller," tradition is strong. When any but the traditional meaning of *chisos* is suggested, the reply is likely to be, "Well, I always heard it means 'ghost.' " This folk meaning seems based on a localized Spanish usage in north-central Mexico, found particularly in the Ojinaga-Presidio area. In this region today, Spanish *chisos* suggests a concept which until recently has been translated into English usually as "ghosts." No example of the singular form, *chiso*, has been found with this meaning.

Leonard Wiley of Presidio observes that from el *hechicero* (sorcerer) comes dialectal *el chiso*, meaning "evil spell" cast by a *chicero*. A local Spanish term, *el chiso* is not infrequently used by Mexicans in Presidio and Ojinaga, but it does not mean any sort of "ghost."

To the Mexican-Americans of the Big Bend the word *chisos* today designates something like a savage, Indian-like bogy-man or spook. *Los chisos* suggests an indescribable, supernatural menace with predatory Apache traits. Apparently the word is so thought of by Mexican children, for as a child Miss Delfina Franco of Presidio used *los chisos* in this sense, as did her playmates. While her mother, Mrs. Lucy Franco, had always understood *los chisos* to mean "Indians," the daughter says, "*Chisos* means something like 'bogy-man.' "

A clear example of the more recently developed meaning was observed in 1946 by Mrs. Hope Tarwater at the picturesque and haunted adobe ruin of Fort Leaton a few miles down the Rio Grande from Presidio. Mexican workers hired by her husband, Mack Tarwater, spoke of mysterious white turkeys they saw flying over the fort at night. When asked why they stopped sleeping on the porch and moved their cots into the field, they explained that evil spirits in the old fort had been turning their beds around.

One day Mrs. Tarwater was at Fort Leaton with two

Mexican boys, fourteen-year-old Chapo Brito and his cousin. When she saw them walking toward town, she called in Spanish: "Chapo, where are you going?"

Chapo said, "My cousin has to go to the dentist. I am afraid to stay here alone. I don't like the ugly noises." His phrase was *los ruidos feos.*

As there were chores to do, Mrs. Tarwater reasoned, "I have to stay here by myself, and I don't mind."

Chapo replied, "But you don't see the *chisos!* (*No ve los chisos!*)"—and away he went with his cousin to the dentist, confident that his gringa boss was immune to visitation by evil spirits that assail the Mexican's peace of mind. But to Chapo, *los chisos* were something that he could see, though vaguely, and that he could most certainly hear.

Many stories of witchcraft and ghosts are set in the Chisos Mountains. These tales seem to deal almost entirely with the protection of buried treasure by evil spirits.

Perhaps some of the legendary lost hordes of silver came from the Lost Chisos Mine, somewhere in these mountains. It is said to have been worked by prisoners brought from the Presidio de San Vicente, just south of the Chisos Mountains on the Mexican ˙ide of the Rio Grande. Blindfolded, the prisoners were marched across miles of hot, rough country to the mine and never permitted to see where they were going. Though none of the prisoners ever returned from the mine, there seems to be no legend current that the mountains are haunted by these men who died laboring inside the earth. However, a familiar tradition has it that if one stands at the entrance of the San Vicente Mission on Easter morning the first rays of the sun will strike the Chisos Mountains at the very spot where the Lost Chisos Mine is located.

At the foot of the highest peak in the Chisos, Mount Emory, is a "lost treasure cave." A long time ago, Spaniards with twenty burro loads of silver were attacked by Indians while coming out of Mexico. The mule drivers raced into the

Chisos Mountains for cover but found themselves in a box canyon. The only escape lay in abandoning the silver and scaling the cliffs. Hastily they hid the silver at the base of a waterfall and climbed to safety.

Their intention was to come back at a later time and recover their cache. But before the luckless Spaniards could return, a rockslide buried the silver. Just where this silver is located, nobody is quite sure. It may be on Lost Mine Peak or it may be at the foot of Mount Emory.

Witchcraft enters the lost treasure story at the Mount Emory setting. It is said that a Mexican and his wife, trudging a cross-country trail to Presidio, once discovered a rich cache of silver bars in a cave at the foot of the peak. Each lifted up two bars of the treasure, and they continued their march homeward, intending to return for the rest. To the wife's sorrow, her husband died on the trail, undoubtedly a victim of the evil spirit in charge of guarding this particular treasure. The woman, however, brought her two bars of silver to Presidio unharmed by the demon and there told her story.

Since the woman would not go back to that tragic place, others went seeking the treasure. They found that before their arrival the evil spirit had let the roof of the cave fall, covering the treasure with tons of rock. (Incidentally, there actually is such a cave with a fallen roof at the base of Mount Emory.) As for the woman's silver bars, some disbelievers say they must have been only lead bars intended for making bullets.

Tales of witchcraft in the Chisos have been used to support the theory that the name is derived from *hechizo,* or "bewitched." In 1953 Walter Fulcher wrote down a tale which runs thus.

> When [the Big Bend] country still belonged to Spain, a party of men were forced to leave the Chisos Mountains and leave behind a large amount of gold. The details are not clear as to whether these men had stolen the gold and were in hid-

ing or whether this is connected with the more famous story of the Lost Chisos Mine. It seems more clear that they had to leave because of the danger of the Indians.

At any rate, they hid the money in a cave. Now one of the men was a *brujo or hechicero,* that is, a wizard who could cast spells and charms, and before they left the cave he made his incantations and cast a spell that no one could break but him.

Invoking the Powers of Darkness, he fixed it so that no one could take the gold away until he returned.

On the way out the party was almost entirely wiped out by Indians. The *hechicero,* whose charms didn't seem to work against Indian arrows, was among those killed.

The survivors told the story, and later some of them returned. Others also tried to carry the gold away but the magic of the dead wizard still held. Some managed to enter the cave, but none could pick up the gold. Thus the mountain came to be called *Cerro del Hechizo,* which in time was shortened to *Chizo* and later applied to the whole mountain range and called *Chisos.*

The story persists to this day. One old Mexican told me, with a perfectly straight face, that once while hunting deer he found the cave with stacks of gold bars, but when he stooped to pick one up he was almost paralyzed and couldn't straighten up. In terror, he managed to creep out of the cave and never went back. Another old Mexican, now so feeble he can hardly walk, assures me that with a rosary and cross and certain words of prayer that only he knows, he can overcome the Powers of Darkness and carry away the treasure, bewitched or not.

As for the ghosts that haunt the Chisos Mountains, one finds, as might be expected, that the area is frequently visited by La Llorona, perhaps the most universal of all Mexican ghosts. This is the "wailing woman" who, after drowning her babies in the Rio Grande so that she might live a wanton life, has been condemned to roam up and down the river for all eternity, weeping and seeking the unabsolved souls of her children. The reason given for the absence of human habitation in the area of San Vicente is, "Nobody will live there because of La Llorona."

Perhaps the best-known purely local ghost legend is that

of Alsate, the last of the Chisos Apaches. This tale was first published in Fort Stockton by Judge O. W. Williams in a privately printed pamphlet. The judge heard the story in 1902 from Natividad Luján of San Carlos, Mexico. It seems that in San Carlos in 1882 Lionicio Castillo betrayed the renegade Chisos Apache chief Alsate to Mexican officials, who marched the chief and his tribesmen into slavery in southern Mexico. (In an interview Alsate's grandson told Glenn Burgess that his bloodthirsty ancestor fell before a firing squad in San Carlos.) The rumor whispered among Big Bend sheepherders and vaqueros soon was that the ghost of Alsate had returned to his old haunts. The ghost was seen wandering in Los Chisos and also in the neighboring Del Carmen Mountains. Most often it was seen standing on some rocky point, looking down upon the rushing waters of the Rio Grande.

Investigating Mexican officials discovered moccasin tracks that led nowhere. In a cave they found animal bones, fresh ashes, and a grass bed, all of which suggested somebody hiding out there—but these were not ghost signs. Nevertheless, natives frequently saw the ghost near this cave. As the phantom apparently was harmless, officials stopped their inquiries, but Castillo, the informer, left the country in terror.

No sooner had Castillo gone than the ghost ceased to appear. With the spirit at peace, Castillo returned, but his neighbors again reported movements of the restless Apache. This time Castillo disappeared, never to be seen again.

As James Cooper of Snyder heard it, Castillo himself had a harrowing vistation. One night, traveling through the Chisos, Castillo made his bed in a roomy cave. As he lay on the cold ground watching the moonlit peaks, he thought of his betrayal of the marauding chief. He laughed to think of Alsate's oath of vengeance upon him. Alsate was dead!

Then Castillo rolled over to view the cold form of the mountain on the other side. There, carved in its ridge, were the exact, terrifying features of Alsate's face. Castillo turned again to face the rear of the cave, to rid his mind of the illusion. Now he heard the winds shrieking among the rocks with the voice of Alsate crying out for his soul.

Rushing from the cave in horror, the informer ran to his house in San Carlos. Even here he was not safe. Whenever he ventured from the village Alsate's spirit appeared. Day by day Castillo grew more fearful and at length disappeared for all time.

The spirit world keeps no secret about the mountainous form of Alsate's ghost. As Los Chisos are entered from the north, Alsate's profile can be seen clearly on the right of the road through the gulch the traveler must follow. The mountain is said to have taken the shape of Alsate's face after his death, so that he might fulfill his vow of revenge upon Lionicio Castillo.

Two lesser-known ghost legends have to do with Indians and bandits in Los Chisos. The legend of Agua Fría Cliff, as told by Isidoro Salgado of Alpine, deals with an Indian woman of the Chisos Mountains whose baby unfortunately was born at the foot of the cliff when the moon was full. The other women reminded her that everybody knew how a baby born under the ill omen of a full moon was sure to turn into some kind of animal—perhaps a coyote or a lizard.

To save her baby an ill fate and herself the shame, the mother carried it up to the edge of Agua Fría Cliff. In her arms the infant moved against her body as she listened to the water bubbling from the rocks below and as she noticed on the cliff the familiar paintings of deer and horses in red and brown. She held her squirming baby with two hands over the cliff, shut her eyes, let go, and closed her ears.

In 1954 Isidoro and his brother-in-law were working cattle near Agua Fría Cliff. Here, he said, "at night the wind seems to be mysterious, because the running water is like singing, when an angel is going to heaven."

After supper one evening as the boys slept on the ground, a noise frightened the horses. Isidoro's kinsman told him,

"The horses are scared of something, because all the time I have been working here, they have acted like something was running after them."

Then Isidoro heard a cry in the darkness. It was the scream of a baby, as though it were falling down the cliff to its death. He told how he had heard this wailing at Agua Fría Cliff again and again. "His crying lasts for a few seconds," he said, "and then it stops." Isidoro Salgado concluded, "I did not believe in ghosts, but I was scared. Now that I have heard this cry, I am convinced that these legends that have been told are true."

Another tale, dealing directly with the origin of the name Los Chisos, was heard by Lawrence Hardin of Crane. A caravan of Mexican traders with mules and two-wheeled carts camped one night by a waterfall and pool at the base of the dark Chisos. These traders passed up and down the Comanche Trail dealing in goods and slaves with frontier Mexican villagers in San Vicente, San Carlos, Lajitas, and Terlingua. While camped, they heard the wind's moaning between the rocks around the waterfall and knew the sound to be the ghost-cry of a girl who died a violent death in these mountains. Therefore they named the mountains "Los Chisos," meaning "The Ghosts."

The girl was the beautiful daughter of a wealthy don who kept an extensive ranch in Mexico. One day bandits descended on the ranch headquarters, looted the house, killed the old man and the servants, and seized the girl. They sat her on a horse and galloped away with her to the Big Bend country. As they rode in hot clouds of dust across the rocky desert, they boasted of how they all would take their pleasure from her body. The girl rode in silence and in tears.

After splashing across the Rio Grande, they took her to a hideout by a pool of water in a lush ravine. At last the desperados dismounted in the grove of live oaks moving in the breeze. The grass, the flowers, and the shade along the water made a luxurious world, foreign to the hot, bright desert only a few yards away. From the mossy rocks fell a sparkling waterfall, surging the stream into white foam.

The sweat-dripping bandits, white dust caked on their eye lashes, restlessly approached the girl, who sat exhausted on her horse by the pool. As the horse drank long swallows of water, one of the bandits put out a hand to drag her from the saddle.

"I am tired," she said. "So warm, so dirty. I am your prisoner. Only let me bathe. Then do with me what you will."

The bandits shrugged, joked, and let the girl dismount and approach the pool. As they smoked and bantered about what they would do to their beautiful captive, they heard her wade into the water.

After a time that seemed too long for their lust, they strode to the water's edge to demand that she come out. There floated the dead, drowned body of the beautiful girl they had brought so far. As the bandits stood amazed a low cry came from under the rocks around the pool. It rose to a blood-freezing scream that bored into their ears. In shriveled fright the bandits scrambled to their horses and fled, leaving the dead girl to float above the bright sand and leaving the rocks howling her vengeance at them.

So it is today when the hot day winds and the cold night winds twist and cry among the mountain rocks. It is Los Chisos.

4.

Old Fort Leaton

NINE miles down the Rio Grande from Presidio, where the dry Alamito Creek joins the river, the ruined adobe walls of Fort Leaton stand. This old private fort is a relic of one of the bloodiest sagas in western American lore. Now partially restored, it is a Texas State Historical Site. In shape the forty rooms sprawl as a squared U with a long base, the front looking out across the old river bank to where the river long ago took a new course. On the north side is a corral inside the U, its connecting wall fallen and gone. Because the tale of Fort Leaton is mostly folklore and scant on fact, it is hard to draw the line between history and frontier gossip in the telling. The story is a two-family saga of land grabbing, assassination, and revenge.

Documents exhumed by Leavitt Corning, Jr. in San Antonio serve well to show how much distance the legends put between themselves and what really happened. In 1848 Ben Leaton bought the *fortín* and adjoining land from Juan Bustillos, with Ed Hall signing as a witness. The boundaries coincided roughly with those of land bought in 1833 by Juana Pedraza, then age twenty-one, but her title was unclear and finally invalidated. A large building already was on the spot when Leaton moved in. Official complaints document Leaton's alleged trading of firearms to Indians for stolen livestock. Leaton died in 1851 in San Antonio ·(as Jerry Sullivan discovered). Juana was left with his three children—Joe, Elizabeth (Isabella), and Bill (Will) Shepard Leaton—and constant money problems. She married Ed Hall, described by a U.S. Army officer as a "villain who is said to be the leader of that gang [of robbers]." When Confederate troops were camped at Fort Leaton in 1861, Joe Leaton and five soldiers tried to kidnap A. W. Wulff in Presidio del Norte (now Ojinaga), and in the fight two Confederate soldiers and one Mexican were killed. Joe said he was taking Wulff to the American side to sign a "document for lands belonging to Mr. E. Hall, Joe Leaton, and orphan children." But what are the facts concerning the alleged tempest of ill will and the murders of Ben Leaton, Ed Hall, and John Burgess? Frontier gossips and the descendants of the main contenders continually alter the saga and fill in the historical gaps with vividly imagined scrapes and killings.

It is impossible to tell this story without weaving threads of history into its fabric. The saga begins before 1846 in the desert and cactus country of West Texas and New Mexico. A former scalp hunter and now an Apache trader, Ben Leaton for some time had planned to settle near the abandoned Fortín de San José, said to be built upon the older ruin of a mission established by the Spaniards about 1690. Leaton was to erect his own fort on a nearby location with materials taken from Fortín de San José. At the present time there lies east and across the creek from Fort Leaton an old adobe and stone foundation, which the Mexicans call El Fortín Viejo ("The Old Fort") to distinguish it from the present ruin of Fort Leaton, which they call El Fortín. Here Dr. Henry Connelly's wagons camped in 1839, when the traveling doctor apparently was the first to try opening the Chihuahua Trail, a route to reduce the distance from San Antonio to Chihuahua by cutting short of the Santa Fe Trail. Never as popular as the longer trail, the Chihuahua Trail had to content itself with a moderate increase in traffic until its decline after the coming of the railroads in the 1880s. As described by August Santleben, one of its regular freighters, the Chihuahua Trail ran from San Antonio to Chihuahua by way of Del Rio, Fort Lancaster (near Sheffield), Horsehead Crossing (near McCamey), Fort Stockton, Paisano Pass (between Alpine and Marfa), Presidio, and the Conchos River roads southwestward in Mexico.

The story goes that hope for development of the Chihuahua Trail was a prime reason that Leaton settled where he did. The location he expected would boom into a major trading and export-import point along the route. Besides, he was tired of bumping over the plains in a rickety wagon, swapping tobacco and gingham to Apaches for stolen mules. Right here Ben Leaton was going to squat, after he had grubstaked himself by marrying Juana Pedraza, a rich Castillian widow of Chihuahua with kin in Presidio del Norte. Here they could sit in one place, buying stolen mules that the Apaches drove into Texas and selling them to freighters driving up and down the trail. They would call the place Fort Leaton. They could irrigate fields in the river bottom and raise corn, beans, and children.

Ben Leaton was said to be among those renegades abhorred by Indian agent James S. Calhoun when he reported from Santa Fe, "For a long time the Prairie Tribes have been supplied with arms and ammunition by the traders on the frontiers of Texas." He said these *comancheros* furnished "five-sixths of the freighter's mules, all of which had been stolen in Mexico" by Indians. Trailed by herds of stolen pack animals, these traders alone could travel freely without danger from the savages. "The whole object of these people," said Calhoun, "is to keep American settlers out of the country as long as possible." Their aim was to continue "their frauds upon the Indians" and to cover 'the most desirable spots with fictitious land-grants." He concluded, "It is through the medium of *these traders* that arms and ammunition are supplied to the Indians who refuse submission to our authority."

According to the tales, when the Mexican War broke out in 1846, Ben Leaton was caught in New Mexico. His train was

loaded with trade goods, which he wanted to drive to Chihuahua and Parras, but the war had cut him off. As the Mexicans
held Santa Fe and El Paso, scores of wagoners were trapped
in the same way, with mules to feed and goods they could not
deliver.

Then General Sterling Price, leading an expedition from
Missouri, captured Santa Fe and marched on to California,
leaving the town in the hands of Colonel Alexander Doniphan
and his Missouri Volunteers. Good news came to the freighters
when they learned that Colonel Doniphan was moving out,
first to capture El Paso del Norte and then to report in Chihuahua to General John E. Wool, U.S.A., who was marching
toward that city at the head of an American invasion force.
Loaded with C.O.D. orders to deliver south of the Rio Grande,
the wagoners trailed Doniphan's column with an eye on the
Mexican trade.

Soon Leaton and Hall were put to work, along with the
other uninvited mule skinners. The colonel formed what he
called the Traders Company, placing it under the command
of Henry Skillman, himself a trader and the elected captain
of his *compadres*. Among these freighters were several men
who were to figure again in the life of Ben Leaton—Larkin
Landrum, Henry Daly, and the wagoner who was to play one
of the darkest roles in the saga of Fort Leaton, John D. Burgess. Leaton's name does not appear on the roster of the Traders Company.

Doniphan's army struggled through its first *jornada del
muerto* ("death journey"), those waterless days from Santa
Fe to El Paso, supposedly with Leaton, Burgess, and the others trailing along. The El Pasoans celebrated the arrival of
the wagons with fiesta and fandango. The traders did a brisk
business in the plaza, where they set up their wares.

Then they pushed on to Chihuahua, through an even
longer death journey than that to El Paso. Fighting alongside
the Missouri Volunteers in a hot skirmish, Leaton and the
other wagoners helped capture Chihuahua. Freighters deliv-

ered their orders, collected their cash, and set up goods for
sale in the plaza while fiesta and fandango were repeated.

Now bad news swept through the Traders Company. Ben
Leaton joined in the general discovery that Colonel Doniphan
had no authority to mobilize the wagoners and that none of
them would be paid. Apparently Ben, Ed Hall, John Burgess,
and the others had fought as hard as the regulars, without a
cent for their pains. Tradition brands Ben Leaton a deserter,
but how could a man desert from an army that didn't exist?
The wagoners, however, continued to follow Doniphan's column for mutual protection, and Ben Leaton proceeded with
them to Parras.

It was May of 1847. As in Chihuahua, some of the Americans tried to drink up all the liquor in town. A group of rowdy
gringos seized a Mexican, accused him of stealing, and tied
him to a tree for flogging. The Mexican was rescued by U. S.
Army officers, and the affair was recorded by Josiah Gregg in
his diary. Gregg added, "Some other outrages were . . . feared
—especially from a desperado by name of Ben Leaton and his
clan; yet, by prompt measures they were checked."

After concluding his affairs in Parras, they say, Ben Leaton returned to Chihuahua, where he married Doña Juana
Pedraza. It seems that Leaton wanted her money and that
she wanted Ben to make her more. She lived in a land where
a great occasion for fiesta was the arrival of traders with their
wagons of imported finery, their young men from the States,
and their Mexican mule-drivers. It was a country where laws
governing the wagon trade were so complicated that officials
were willingly lax for a price. Then, having taken a bribe from
a trader, the official might accept another from bandits in exchange for information about the trader's arms, goods, and
route.

Doña Juana set up her new husband with a trading post
where he would rule the only settlement between El Paso and
Eagle Pass. She bought a crumbling, old building that would
become a castle for herself and an armed fortress for them

both. This would be the first private fortress in the region, followed in 1849 by Fort Cíbolo, built by the rancher Milton Faver near Shafter. When completed, the roof was protected by a crenelated parapet, so that defenders could fight off besiegers.

When the commercial arrangement was firm, John Burgess and Larkin Landrum were included in it with Ben Leaton and Ed Hall. Leaton was to be law in the Big Bend, with Fort Leaton as his headquarters and trading center. Fort Leaton controlled the Chihuahua Trail where, approaching from the north, it crossed Alamito Creek to arrive at the fort, then crossed the Rio Grande into Mexico. With Ben Leaton as the only "customs official," Burgess was to set up his freight wagon headquarters and store on the flat-topped hill south of the river in Presidio de Norte. Ed Hall was to serve as Leaton's right-hand man at the fort. Henry Daly acquired a ranch where Presidio, Texas, now stands, and Landrum operated a ferry. Apparently this crew concurred with the idea that partners don't have to love each other if they all love money.

In the summer of 1847 the Leaton and Burgess wagons bumped the hundred and fifty rocky miles from Chihuahua northward along the Rio Conchos valley trail toward the Rio Grande. The Leatons would stay in Presidio del Norte with Doña Juana's relatives until the ruin was made habitable. After they moved into the high-walled spaciousness of the adobe fort, Doña Juana, sitting in her rocking chair on the porch facing the Rio Grande, could look across to the Mexican side and see El Cerrito de la Santa Cruz with its rustic stone chapel and three crosses, which by their spell kept the devil in his cave. It had been a century and a half since Juan Sabeata said he saw the burning cross in the heavens above this hill.

Legend says that in order to get his Indian trade going Leaton promoted private relations with a barbecue. He sent out runners to invite the Indians to a feast at his newly established fort. His men and women, many said to be Indian

slaves, ground corn for tortillas and set deer and antelope car-
casses to roasting in the huge fireplace. Wine and grape
brandy were plentiful, brought down the river from El Paso
vineyards. Along the sunbaked trails came Apaches, Comanches, and Kiowas, including the women, and also American
and Mexican blood-brothers. In the Indians' herds ran horses
scarred with brands to be found in the Bexar County Brand
Book. Unwritten peace and trade agreements with predatory
Indians were enjoyed already by such neighboring Mexican
villages as San Carlos, San Vicente, Boquillas, and Presidio
del Norte. Ben was about to make a similar deal for his Fort
Leaton on the American side.

Expecting guests, Ben supervised the meat sizzling above
the embers, the bubbling pots of beans, and the goatskins
swelling with liquor. That night the moon shone and torches
blazed on the adobe-walled plaza. Grazing together on the
bunch grass on the plain north of the fort were mustangs and
mules belonging to Leaton and the Indians. Leaton greeted
the chiefs, probably including Gómez in his silver-buckled
leggins, a lace mantilla tied around his waist, moccasins on his
feet, a dusty beaver hat on his head, and a colorful, dirty
serape over his shoulder. Perhaps Santiago was there too.
Everybody spoke the mutilated Spanish of the Comanche
Trail, the Indians' diplomatic lingua franca used to bridge the
multitude of native dialects.

There was nothing complicated about the deal Leaton
wished to make. He wanted friendly relations with the Indians. The Indians could exchange their stolen livestock for
knives, liquor, and money at Fort Leaton. They liked to have
silver coins with which to decorate their clothes. Leaton could
sell the mules and horses at a profit to the army and to freight
wagon bosses. The Indians would wish to sell Leaton some
of the women and children they captured, but like other
comancheros Leaton would buy only those he knew he could
make a profit on by ransoming them to their families. (The
story goes that he bought and enslaved some captives any-

way, and that he stocked a harem in this manner. Some say Leaton's captives were kept in a windowless cell and that food was shoved to them through a small opening in the wall.)

In the parley Leaton played his highest card when he offered to sell guns, powder, and lead to the Indians. It had been the Indians' custom to hide their firearms in Texas before crossing the Rio Grande, the lance and arrow being the only weapons needed against the Mexicans, who were legally prohibited from bearing arms. By this time, however, a new factor had intruded. Governor Angel Trias of Chihuahua was paying a bounty for Indian scalps, and the Indians needed guns to fight scalp-hunting parties led by James Kirker and John Glanton.

When the feast was over, Leaton had come to terms with the Indians, as far as he could tell. That night he fastened the bar on the wagon door to his corral and watched the Indians gallop away to their camps. Out in the pasture his own stock stood grazing in the moonlight.

Next morning when Ben opened the wagon door, his jaw dropped. His eyes scoured the plain northward to the Chinati Mountains. Every single horse and mule he owned was gone. Ben reverted to the vicious old sentiment "The only good Indian is a dead one."

Soon, however, Leaton led the Indians to believe that he could take a joke—this horse thieving—and kept up his trade with them. He put out an invitation to a second barbecue but meanwhile had his wagons fetch him a second-hand cannon, complete with powder and grapeshot, from Chihuahua. Again torches blazed in the patio and the coals sizzled beneath the blacktail deer in preparation for what legend calls the Second Housewarming.

Circling through the house, Leaton took his stand behind a falsely walled-off portion of the patio, where the cannon stood. His men helping him, he toppled the adobe wall and lit the big gun. In the roar and smoke, flame, blood, and wine ran together. Screaming savages reeled and fell, mingled with the roasted legs of wild animals. Through their screams another blast roared from the cannon. Then Leaton and his men finished the live ones with their knives. Chihuahua paid well for scalps.

It seems indisputable that this tale about the Second Housewarming is a variation of an actual incident in the life of Ben Leaton. In 1837 he was a scalp hunter in New Mexico with John Johnson and was present at the so-called Santa Rita Massacre, in which Johnson is said to have lured Indians into camp only to mow them down with chain shot from a cannon concealed under a pile of saddles. In the retelling, Ben Leaton has taken the leading role and the story moved from place to place with Leaton.

Legend does not date these yarns about the rough Indian diplomacy of Ben Leaton. History, however, indicates that he built faith in his future prosperity on obvious official interest in making Fort Leaton an important point on a road from San Antonio to El Paso. In 1848 and the year following, Fort Leaton had two important sets of visitors, the first by official action from Austin, the second on orders from the U. S. Army. As recorded in history, Ben Leaton did what he could to entertain and assist his important callers, no doubt with hope of strengthening the case for the new El Paso road.

In the summer of 1848, Jack Hays and his Chihuahua–El Paso Expedition arrived to find Fort Leaton "a sort of fortified trading house kept by two or three brothers of that name." While there, the Hays party was treated to a barbecue at which mainly meat, tortillas, and coffee were served. They remained sixteen days "recruiting" their animals and putting in supplies, some of which were sent to them by the bishop of Chihuahua. It seems that on his return trip to San Antonio, Hays brought a small son of Leaton to be placed in school.

Perhaps the most detailed account of the Leatons and the fort is that by Lieutenant William Whiting. His mission was to explore the feasibility of making the fort a point on a new trail from San Antonio to El Paso. On the morning of March

24, 1849, the "jaded spirits" of Whiting and his men were lifted by their "view of the Rio Grande with its green valley and cottonwood groves." Whiting said, "At seven we reached Fort Leaton, where we received a warm welcome and great hospitality. Leaton has performed severe labor and has gone to much expense in his location. His fort is a collection of adobes . . . with a lookout and a wall which encloses also his corral. The rooms are surmounted by a crenelated parapet wall, and the place would make a strong defense against Indians. He represents those living between this and the Paso as hostile in the extreme." Hospitable and cooperative, Leaton let Whiting and his party camp in his yard, had firewood brought, and saw that "an enormous dinner" was served to the soldiers. Whiting says Leaton had about ten Americans working for him and that he ran a fairly successful farming operation. For the next few days the expedition rested while their purchase of dried beef, cornmeal, and pinole—"parched corn ground and sweetened, a very pleasant and nutritive article of food" —was prepared. The lieutenant observed that prices were high.

In view of Leaton's reputation as a horse trader, it is thought-provoking to notice that Whiting said, "We will require many new animals," but did not state how many he acquired or where they came from. He said only, "Leaton is very active and enterprising in his assistance. His endeavors with small resources to promote our success lay me under many obligations."

In his report Whiting urged that the chief of engineers establish a permanent trail through Fort Leaton westward. He said that the fort was "one of the most important places on the Rio Grande" because of its position favorable not only to trade in the southwestern territories and in Mexico but also to the military's quelling of hostile Indians.

While at Fort Leaton, Whiting visited Presidio del Norte, and he mentioned the desolate aspect of that "collection of one-story adobe buildings . . . on one of the gravel tables at the junction of the Conchos and the Rio Grande." The fortress was a "rude adobe structure, oblong in shape . . . containing the church and the barracks." The five or six hundred men under Commandant Don Guillermo Ortiz were "miserable, ragged creatures apparently half starved and called 'soldiers.'" A scarecrow of a sentry walked up and down bearing "a bankrupt escopette." The well-mannered commandant, however, after a round of whiskey and El Paso brandy, treated his guests to a dinner of chicken stewed in chile sauce, tortillas, roasted turkey, frijoles, and coffee, served one course at a time.

About a week later, as Whiting's force disappeared up the trail along the river toward El Paso, Leaton's hope for the establishment of a road by way of his fort traveled with them. Despite Whiting's recommendation, however, the road took a more northerly course. Fort Leaton's importance was stunted almost before it had any chance to grow. It was to remain an isolated, by-passed border settlement with little history and less prosperity.

Trouble came from Chihuahua and even from Washington, D.C., for both governments disapproved of Leaton's law in the Big Bend. Governor Trias of Chihuahua complained to Major Jefferson Van Horne in El Paso that Leaton was a troublemaker. From the American side the major received a similar complaint from the Army Inspector General's Department. Leaton was accused of providing the Indians with arms used against Americans and of buying from them animals and goods stolen from Mexican citizens. Major General George M. Brooke, commander of the Eighth Corps Area, wrote from his stone quadrangle in San Antonio instructing Major Van Horne to inform Governor Trias that action had been taken to put Leaton in his place.

Finding himself under fire, Leaton bumped with his wagons up the Chihuahua Trail to explain his position. Besides this, he could bring merchandise for trade. He also brought his wife and children on the first leg of his journey, toward a vacation in New Orleans. In San Antonio, General Brooke may have told Leaton that because of his selling guns to the Indians travelers had a hazardous journey across the Trans-Pecos country. He could have told him, further, that the State of Texas had given up trying to organize Presidio County because of Indian wildness that he was partly responsible for. Leaton is almost sure to have replied that the general could not understand the situation in the Big Bend because he was too far away from it. Nevertheless, after he was reprimanded, Leaton continued on his way.

At this point in the saga, history abandons Fort Leaton and legend takes up the story almost altogether, casting it into a murk of inconsistency. One tale says that Ben Leaton was proprietor of Fort Leaton until he was murdered, another says he died of malaria in New Orleans in 1851, and yet another that malaria got him in Galveston, where he was delivering cattle. (The fact is that he died in San Antonio about August 1, 1851, nobody knows how.) Tangent tradition holds that Ben Leaton never even existed. Others say that the owner of the fort was called Ed Leaton and that Ben was Ed's eldest, mentally retarded son, who died in San Antonio in 1930, also of malaria. Then who was Ed Hall, whose presence in the saga is as important as that of Ben Leaton? What of the tradition that the three children of Doña Juana—Bill, Isabella, and Joe—each had a different father, yet all were surnamed Leaton?

According to the main line of the saga, Ben Leaton, Apache trader from Tennessee (or maybe Kentucky, Virginia, or Victoria, Texas) was very much alive in 1853 (though in fact he had been dead for more than a year). He was running a comfortable plantation on the Rio Grande. He occupied an adobe house he had built about four hundred yards east of the trading post, and here he and his family enjoyed privacy apart from the fort, which housed American employees, Mexican servants, and laborers. His irrigation ditches watered his river bottom farms. The shelled corn made perfect barter goods in trading with the Apaches during the winter hunger, as well as feed for his own horses and mules.

But not all was solid comfort. From across the Rio Grande, John Burgess began to cast a covetous eye. Both Burgess and his wife were of a wild disposition, and Burgess was eager to gobble up Leaton's fort and make himself the trading tycoon of the Big Bend. Then Burgess is said one day to have killed a Mexican held in some esteem by the townsmen. Whatever the cause, Burgess and his family left Presidio del Norte and took up quarters at Fort Leaton.

At least the Leatons had the peace of their separate house while the temperamental Burgesses screamed at each other in the fort. One night, however, as Ben Leaton sat down to supper with his family, John Burgess sneaked through the dark, his fingers grasping a pistol. With customary caution Leaton had placed himself at the table so as to be watching the back door, which could let in trouble as well as friends. The back door burst open, the silhouette of John Burgess pointed a pistol, and Isabella jumped to protect her father. Blasting flame streaked into the kitchen, and Ben Leaton slumped dead in his chair, shot through the chest. Little Bill and Joe yelled with terror, and blood streamed from the side of little Isabella. Burgess backed into the darkness, the pistol in his hand.

While this story may be plausible enough, Joe Larkin Burgess told Mabel Lowry in 1969 that his grandfather had nothing to do with the death of Ben Leaton. According to Burgess family tradition, Ben Leaton owed money to two Germans in Ojinaga. When they came to the fort one night to collect, the argument turned into a brawl in which Leaton was shot and killed. A young woman called Chata leaped with a straight razor to cut the throat of one of the debt collectors but only wounded his chin. The Germans lit out to Parras and were not heard from again.

Regardless of how Leaton died in legend, it is with his death that the story of feuding and land grabbing starts. Most versions take Ed Hall's marriage to Juana into account and say that sometime after Burgess killed Ben Leaton tempers cooled in Presidio del Norte and Burgess was back there tending store. To hold possession of her property Doña Juana moved back into the fort with her children. As a woman, she could not own the property her husband had acquired with her own money, but she was administrator of the estate for her children. Ed Hall was her manager and advised her concerning their wagon trade and their trade in stolen goods and livestock. Before the end of 1853 she married Ed Hall, and Ed became master of the Leaton estate. But along with the land and the fort, Ed acquired also the envy and hatred of John Burgess.

In 1854 the establishment of Fort Davis, some hundred miles north of Fort Leaton, opened a new market for both Hall and Burgess. The presence of the army caused a slump in trade with the Indians, but if it depressed one market it created another. The calvary post required feed and hay, and its post exchange was an outlet for liquor and trade goods. The calvary needed remounts, and passing wagon trains required draft animals. Also, Fort Davis was a point on the Butterfield Stage line, where Henry Skillman and Big Foot Wallace sometimes rolled in atop the driver's seat. Hall and Burgess hauled corn and beans to Fort Davis to feed the troops. To San Antonio, they hauled saddles and silver, and back to Fort Davis and the Mexican border they brought trade goods. Fort Davis clung to its rocky foothold on the southwestern trail.

With the Civil War, Fort Davis was gradually obliterated. Once the Federal troops moved out, Confederate troops moved in, sustaining the life of the fort and its trade for a short time. It was during this brief occupation that two soldiers were killed in Presidio del Norte while aiding Joe Leaton in his personal vendetta against A. W. Wulff, whom Leaton believed was implicated in Burgess' violent acquisition of Fort Leaton. When the Confederates abandoned Fort Davis, the Indians burned it down and a few survivors walked the hundred miles to Fort Leaton and safety.

The drying up of the Fort Davis trade brought death not only to the Leaton trading post but to Ed Hall as well. Legend says that in 1862 Ed owed Burgess $1,061 and had put up Fort Leaton as security for the loan. His money was out to his enemy, and not a nickel was coming in. Wagons had almost ceased to run, though sometimes Big Foot Wallace came along, prodding a string of pack mules out of Mexico, bound for San Antonio with smuggled coffee and sugar. Sometimes Henry Skillman came through with messages from Confederate agents in Chihuahua to Confederate officials in Austin. Trade was slow in San Antonio and everywhere else that was cut off by the war from Northern manufacture. Meanwhile, John Burgess threatened foreclosure.

Bill and Joe Leaton were no more eager to give up Fort Leaton than their mother and stepfather. Burgess knew that with Fort Davis destroyed there was no semblance of a county judge to enforce the foreclosure of his mortgage against the place. Ed Hall knew that, where there is no law, a man like Burgess makes law and enforces it with his pistol. And Burgess had no doubt that Ed would fight the case with guns himself.

Sleeping in the fort one night Hall awoke to a noise in the patio. Pistol in hand, he stepped out into the night. The moon made a square of light on the ground and black shadows against two walls. Ed knew Burgess was after him. His hair stood on end as young Bill came toward him through the moonlight. A lasso snaked out of the shadow, snared the boy, and dragged him screaming into the dark. Ed cursed his unseen attacker and yelled for a fair chance. He dared not shoot into the dark, not knowing where the boy was. Gunfire ripped out of the shadows, and the corpse of Ed Hall fell to the ground, soaking it with his blood. Burgess had foreclosed.

Doña Juana took her boys across the river to Presidio del

Norte, where she moved in with relatives. Bill Leaton clenched his fist and vowed that when he grew up he would kill the man who had unfathered him twice.

There is disagreement again, this time in conflicting tales of how Ed Hall came to die. Ben's grandson, Victor Leaton Ochoa, told Mrs. Jack Shipman a Leaton family tradition in 1922. He said that after Doña Juana married Ed Hall, "Superintendent of the Overland Stage Line section to El Paso," Hall borrowed $10,000 from John D. Burgess, "a prominent lawyer of San Antonio," and gave him a mortgage on the fort. When Hall failed to pay, two men shot and killed him "sitting at his desk in the room to the east of the main portal door that faces the south." A few days later Burgess and nine other men took possession of the place, he said, adding that Burgess gave Doña Juana $2,000 and that she took her children to Ojinaga.

The two boys vowed revenge on all ten usurpers. "Long before the boys had arrived at legal age," Ochoa went on, "they had killed the nine men. All the killings were done in Ojinaga, where the officials were friends of the Leaton boys and sympathized with them. The boys were never prosecuted." Finally, said Ben Leaton's grandson, John Burgess was killed by Bill Leaton.

People have to get along, even when there is bad blood between them, and the story goes that Doña Juana and her children settled down to an outwardly peaceful life. Burgess weathered the Civil War as master of Fort Leaton, and after the war both Fort Davis and its trade were reactivated. When Captain Mose Kelley was assigned as customs officer in Presidio, Texas, in 1867, Burgess escorted him from El Paso by boat down the Rio Grande. The trip was partly for business, partly for pleasure. In the party, as it swiftly floated between flat deserts and through deep canyons, was young Bill Leaton. His hatred ran like the water of the Rio Grande, sometimes underground.

Some thought the Burgesses might destroy themselves in

their own squalor before Bill had his chance. All were fiery tempered. At meals they flew into a fury and hurled bowls of beans and gravy at each other, slopping up the room until it was a dripping mess. With blood in their eyes, they chased each other screaming and cursing through and around the rambling fort.

They were always ready to defend themselves. A tale has it that one evening when the men were gone, Señora Tomasita Burgess knelt before the hot embers in the fireplace, tending a great iron skillet sizzling with catfish. Silently an Apache crept into the room, arms outstretched to make her a captive. She heard a moccasin shuffle. Quickly she heaved up the skillet, threw boiling grease and fish all over the savage, and then brought the iron pan down on his head. As the Indian writhed on the floor, she pounded his skull until he was dead.

A related story says that on a hog-killing day the Burgesses were rendering a pot of lard over a fire on the patio. When darkness fell they moved the iron pot indoors to the fireplace. Soon they were aware of somebody peeping into the room through a hole in the wall. One of the Burgesses dashed a pan of hot grease through the hole. The next day an Indian, horribly blinded by his burns, was found wandering aimlessly near the fort.

At least once the law had to interfere with the Burgess carryings-on. After the Civil War a semblance of local government developed in the Texas village of Presidio, and the scattered neighbors and ranchers elected Richard C. Daly, a storekeeper, as justice of the peace. Often he was assisted by his son Henry.

One of the sons of John Burgess hung out at a saloon across the river. Behind the bar worked a Mexican against whom young Burgess had developed a grievance. Burgess fired up his wrath one night and put a bullet through the bartender. Like many another desperado, he found it necessary to spend some time in hiding out from the avenging friends of the dead man.

All Presidio was quiet for several days. But the air tightened one afternoon as Justice Daly, standing in front of his general store, saw a cloud of dust sweeping up the road toward him from Fort Leaton. From a sweating horse one of the Burgess girls pleaded with Daly for help. Her murderous brother had come home and was trying to kill his wife.

Daly and his son strapped on their pistols, mounted, and followed the girl back down the river to Fort Leaton. They dismounted, drew their pistols, and followed the girl into the courtyard. The girl motioned toward the door to the room of impending death. Richard Daly took the knob in his hand, his son behind him, and shoved open the door.

In the middle of the bare room the Mexican wife of young Burgess half crouched, tears of terror streaming down her face, and pleaded for her life. His pistol aimed at his wife, young Burgess sat grinning and taunting in a cane-bottomed chair against the opposite wall.

When he saw the two lawmen, Burgess drew a new bead and fired. The bullet smashed into Richard Daly's shoulder and knocked him to one side. Henry Daly pulled his trigger, and in the roar and smoke young Burgess toppled to the floor. The woman ran to stand against the wall near the Daly men. Glassy-eyed, her husband raised himself on an elbow and leveled his pistol again at his wife. Henry Daly sighted on the fallen man's head. But the wavering gun arm sank slowly, and young Burgess relaxed lifeless and bleeding on the floor.

With the years fate was closing in on John D. Burgess, because Bill Leaton was growing up. While the wagoner prospered and his trains furnished supplies to the West Texas forts, Bill's hatred smoldered. In his eighteenth year it blazed out and consumed the man who had killed his father and stepfather, who with knives and guns had stolen his mother's adobe castle. The right time for Bill finally arrived.

One December day in 1875, they say, he learned that Burgess was on the trail to Fort Davis, alone except for his Negro cook. Burgess seems to have made the journey in order to collect four hundred dollars due him in Fort Davis. Bill rode up Alamito Creek. He paused at the San Esteban Water Hole, where the Spanish explorer Augustín Rodríguez had erected a special cross two hundred and fifty years before. Across the highland plain he moved through Paisano Pass into the Davis Mountains. He paused at Burgess Water Hole (now Alpine). He pushed on to Fort Davis and reached the settlement on Christmas Eve.

Somehow Bill Leaton missed his enemy, for John Burgess was now camped for the night by the clear and shallow Musquiz Creek, about twelve miles south of Fort Davis. His four hundred dollars were tucked in a saddlebag under his head.

On Christmas morning Burgess awoke as the bacon sizzled in the Negro's skillet. First thing, he checked on his money, but to his dismay he found only an unbuckled flap on his saddlebag. His temper exploding, he cursed the Negro for a thief and reached for his pistol. Knowing his boss's violence, the Negro leaped on his horse and lit out bareback toward Fort Davis with bullets flying past his head.

Burgess saddled his mount and galloped in pursuit. The Christmas sun was well up when he rode into the village at Fort Davis, a scattering of adobe huts along Limpia Creek. A few Mexicans and fewer Anglos were on the village paths, but they disappeared when Burgess rode into town.

Burgess decided to hunt the Negro first in the low adobe structure that housed the saloon and general store. The saloon door was open, showing only darkness inside. Burgess walked out of the sunlight into the blinding shadows. At the bar a vaguely shadowed man turned to face him. Now he saw it was Bill Leaton, and that Bill had a pistol in his hand. Before Burgess could claw his own pistol out of its holster, a bullet smashed into his chest. He fell to the dirt floor a corpse.

After fourteen years of suppressed hatred, young Leaton had his revenge. From behind the counter rose the bartender and the Negro.

Now to escape the Anglos' law. Bill put away his gun,

ran to his horse, and spurred for Mexico. He dodged the main trail, evading the Americans' law and the Texas Rangers. He celebrated Christmas picking his way along the rougher and less-traveled trail down Cíbolo Creek toward the Rio Grande.

The day after Christmas this trail brought him to the mountains near Shafter, a silver-mining settlement. On top of a mountain a man appeared. His wide sombrero and the flapping blanket over his shoulder showed him to be a Mexican. The man shouted and waved his arms to William. He came running down the slope toward him. Bill stopped. He knew the "Mexican telegraph" carried gossip faster than horses and across unbelievable distances. He knew that his shooting of John Burgess must now be common knowledge throughout the Big Bend. This man dashing down the mountain—was he a friend or was he a decoy setting a trap? Fear swept through Bill like a cold wind; he drew his pistol and killed the approaching Mexican. The body rolled down the slope and stopped against a patch of prickly pear in the rocks.

Bill Leaton spurred his wet horse down the smugglers' trail through the last row of mountains north of Presidio. Now he needed only to cross the cactus-dotted plain to the river. Two or three more hours brought him to the willow and cane brakes along the river, into the Rio Grande, and out of the water on the Mexican side. At a walk Bill took the sandy trail through the willows along the river toward Presidio del Norte. He was almost home.

Suddenly a man stepped out of the willows onto the path. A rifle was in his hands, and brass buttons gleamed on his shirt. It was a soldier. Did they want him for killing Burgess? Did they want him because of the unknown dead man at Shafter? Was the man trying to warn him and turn him back? Now another soldier stepped out of the brush.

Whipping out his pistol, Bill shot down one of the men and plunged his horse squarely into the other, knocking him to the ground. As Bill flew toward Presidio del Norte, the fallen soldier rose from beneath the horse's feet, aimed his rifle between Bill's shoulder blades, and fired. Bill tumbled dead from his horse. The wounded soldier stood, tended his wound, and they both trudged through the sand toward Presidio del Norte. They must inform Doña Juana where the body of her young avenger lay.

This all sounds very like the end of the story, and indeed it may be said that this is the conclusion of the "public legend" dealing with old Fort Leaton. Shot through with historical facts, these legends are fair examples of how the folk imagination insists on filling in the gaps when hard evidence is unobtainable. For the most part the gaps are filled in a way that shows a preference for violence and melodrama on the part of the tale transmitters. Among descendants of both the Leatons and the Burgesses, however, there are stories passed down in family traditions that differ sharply in many ways from the "public" version. Sometimes the stories within the same family take exception to each other on the subject of just how Ben Leaton, John Burgess, and Bill Leaton died.

In 1922 Ben Leaton's grandson told Jack Shipman that on a summer day (not Christmas) John Burgess was drinking in Fort Davis at the store of Sanders and Sedenburn. His wagons already had started homeward, and it was a fairly drunk Burgess who rode out to catch up with them. In half an hour a Mexican came racing his pony into town, Burgess right behind him. The Mexican disappeared among the adobe houses behind O. M. Keesey's general store. In front of the store stood Keesey and Bill Leaton. Burgess reined up and said:

"Hello, Keesey. Did you see that greaser? Where'd he go? I'll kill him. . . . Say, ain't you Bill Leaton?"

"Yes. Ain't you John Burgess?"

Burgess shot Bill Leaton twice in the chest, and Bill shot Burgess five times, right between the eyes, obviously in self-defense. Victor Leaton Ochoa concluded his story, "Keesey, himself being justice of the peace, did not even arrest Bill Leaton—not for killing John G. Burgess."

Continuing in what seems a vein of family partiality, Victor Leaton Ochoa said that his Uncle Bill later killed a Negro sergeant and was sentenced to the penitentiary. He was pardoned by the governor of Texas, however, before serving any of his time. Sometime later he was killed in Ojinaga "in a row in which he first killed three Mexican policemen."

Family traditions on the Burgess side have grown more elaborate with each generation, from the son of John D. Burgess to his grandson. In 1922 Juan Burgess' story varied considerably from anybody else's. He said that in 1848 John D. Burgess came to Presidio with John Spencer's colony and married an Ojinaga girl. (Spencer had been a scalp hunter with James Kirker.) Here it was that Burgess (not Leaton or Bustillos) built the forty-room *fortín* near the farm of Ben Leaton. It was some years later, he said, that "the fort was removed from the top."

From the freighting enterprise, he went on, this respectable John Burgess grew comfortably rich. A native of Virginia, he supported the Southern cause during the Civil War and, generous to a fault, gave away his wealth to Southerners who drifted into the Big Bend. He served the South by freighting supplies to Southern forces and sympathizers at El Paso, and his supply train once was captured by Union soldiers. He escaped, however, and made his way back to the *fortín* on a mule.

As for Ben Leaton (said Burgess' son), he was a bad character who not only traded guns to Indians but rounded up Mexicans and forced them to work on his farm. Later when Ben (not Bill) was on trial for killing John D. Burgess, he killed a Negro soldier and for the two murders was sent to the penitentiary. Juan Burgess gave no details as to how his father died.

A grandson of John D. Burgess, however, in 1969 had a different story. Interestingly enough, here was a Burgess who absolved the Leatons of killing his ancestor. Joe Larkin Burgess told Mabel Lowry that John Burgess was in Fort Davis at Christmastime with his wagons and that he had just been paid in gold coin by the post quartermaster for delivery of supplies. After stuffing the coins in his moneybelt, he and a Negro mule skinner were drinking at a store while the other wagons went ahead. Finally the two drove to a grove about twenty-one miles north of Marfa and pitched camp. When Burgess was asleep the Negro shot him dead, stole the money, and fled to Chihuahua.

Now Vidal Burgess, old John's son, swore vengeance, and the first time he heard the Negro was in Ojinaga, he went for him. When they met, the Negro was on horseback and Vidal was on foot. The Negro shot at Vidal, and hit him in the foot. Vidal fired back, putting five bullets into the Negro's forehead. After Vidal had hastened to the American side, officials got word to him that he would not be arrested in Ojinaga. They were grateful that he had rid the town of a troublemaker. According to Salomón Ramos of Alpine, Vidal afterward was shot and killed by Richard Daly for some violent infraction.

The ruined walls of Fort Leaton stand near Alamito Creek, and the devil grins down from his high cave on the cliff across the Rio Grande. The river has shifted its course southward by a mile, avoiding the tumbled walls. In the private cemetery just north of Fort Leaton, the Burgesses are buried. Beside their graves is an unmarked grave. Does it contain Ben Leaton or Ed Hall or both? Inside the fort the huge fireplace is cold, and the courtyard once sparsely patched with goathead stickerweeds and prickly pear, has been paved by the state.

At night, so the old ones tell, wails of distress rise from the blood-soaked patio. At other times, the shuffle of invisible moccasins whispers about the fatal ground. Also on the patio, on dark nights, a tin can full of money bounces and rolls about in ghostly fashion. Burgesses of a later generation, in the cool of the evening, sometimes saw an empty rocking chair silently swaying of its own accord. Doña Juana comes back in death to claim her adobe castle on the Rio Grande.

5.
Water Witching in the Big Bend

IN the Big Bend water witching is little different from what it is anywhere else, except that the "witches" often use wire rods instead of pliant tree branches for wands. The reason for this is simple. Few trees of any kind grow in the Big Bend, and even fewer like the willow and other so-called witch plants with limber branches. This omission from the landscape proves to the witch that the power to find water by divination or dowsing is in the witch and not in the wand.

In the almost five-hundred-year history of witching there has been no change in technique. The only basic difference now is that the elaborate superstitions that once attended it have been discarded in favor of more simple, rational and scientific explanations of why the wand bends in the witch's hands right over what he is seeking. The uncanny power is said to lie in the extra-sensory perception of the water witch himself. Some claim the facility to be a neurological capacity in some people that is beyond the present knowledge of science.

Associated with divine magic, water witching has nothing to do with witchcraft. Witching derives its name from the kind of tree whose branches provide the limber wands found most suitable for the practice. Many of these are called witch plants, the best known being the witch hazel. In *Beowulf* such a limber tree is a *wic* (probably pronounced "witch"), and Beowulf said *wican* when he meant "bend"; in Chaucer's time this kind of tree was known as a *wiche*. About the only words today to come out of the old vocabulary are *wicker* and *witch* as in water witch.

The long and honorable history of witching goes back to at least 1540, when, in what Herbert C. Hoover said is the earliest published account, Georgius Agricola told of witching for veins of ore in Germany. In 1568 in Spain, Saint Teresa, who needed a water well, saw a Father Antonio make some kind of movement with a twig, after which he said, "Dig here." —"And lo!" said Saint Teresa, "A plentiful fount of water gushed forth." The practice of witching spread to the New World, where it is reputed to be successful more often than not, and has been popular ever since.

Witching looks simple. The witch holds an end of a forked wand in each hand, and when the wand is directly over what he wants to find it dips vigorously, seemingly all by itself with no urging from the witch. In the hands of most people, the rod will not move. Yet, I have held one end of the wand twice, once with Perry Cartwright and once with Beryl Ponton, both of Alpine. In each instance my end of the rod twisted in my hand though my partner's hand did not make a move. Supreme Court Justice William O. Douglas (in Alpine working on a book) told me that he had the same experience, except that, whereas I was holding a wire, he had held one end of a green forked branch. He said, "I held on tight so I could tell if she moved it herself. The twig twisted downward so hard that the bark peeled off in my hand." Judge Douglas' conclusion, like mine, was, "There must be something to it." Neither the judge nor I would ever succeed as a water witch, for the rod will not work for either of us on our own. But there are others in the Big Bend who have been very successful water witches. One of the most notable was The Boy with X-ray Eyes.

Tales about fourteen-year-old Guy Fenley of Uvalde say that he could see right through the surface of the earth to underground water. Sometime in the late 1890s at his father's ranch house, the lad, who was playing on the gallery, leaned over the edge and told his father he could see a clear stream of water running far down under the ground. His unbelieving father simply took it as one of the strangest things he ever heard a mischievous boy say. Then Guy began talking about how he could look through cattle, horses, and people and see their bones as plain as any x-ray machine. Hence the name by which he became known: The Boy with the X-ray Eyes. Riding horseback on the ranch, Guy persisted in seeing underground water until his father, Joel Fenley, decided to settle this wild claim once and for all. It had dawned upon him that he just might have a water witch in the family, and to find out he put Guy and his other boys to work.

First they learned that Guy's x-ray facility worked best at night. In the dark and in territory they knew Guy was unfamiliar with, the brothers sent Guy ahead looking for water. Guy would announce that he had spied an underground stream and would start to follow it. The brothers followed Guy's trail through the mesquite and greasewood, marking his trail and his discoveries with heaps of stones or piles of brush. Then they would conduct the young diviner by a devious, circuitous route back to the starting place and put him to the test by starting out again to trace the same alleged underground stream. The brothers swore that Guy always would follow the same trail exactly, in the dark sometimes stumbling over the rock and brush piles that marked his first go-round.

It was in the Big Bend canyon country that Guy Fenley was put to the supreme test. Two of his brothers owned a waterless ranch on the Rio Grande, where from the edge of the pasture to the river it was a sheer drop of several hundred feet. With no way for either people or cows to get to the water, the brothers needed a well desperately and were ready for Guy to locate one if he could.

Having set up camp, the party headed out in the night, the boy leading the way. Soon he saw a sparkling stream of water running down in the earth. He walked with his eyes

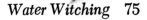

half closed, peering right through the earth's crust at his find, stepping along and announcing the depth. At first he judged the water to be five hundred feet down, but before long he announced that it was getting nearer the surface. "Now it's two hundred feet to the water," he said. Apparently he walked as though moving along the bank of the stream he spied. When he bumped into obstructions like clumps of prickly pear, he would turn aside and make a jump as though springing across a brook. "Now about a hundred and fifty," he said, and having taken a few more paces he stopped.

"The water is about eighty feet below the surface here, but it drops over a high precipice and a few steps farther goes down, down." He advanced several yards and announced, "It's five hundred feet to the water here."

Calling it a hopeful night's work, the men took Guy back to camp and turned in. When they got a drilling rig to the spot Guy chose and started punching, Guy reportedly foretold the various kinds of rock, gravel, and dirt formations the bit successively struck. Guy passed his first test with honors, for a fine stream of clear water was struck at eighty-one feet. It should be noted here that implicit in the account of his first water-finding venture is Guy's ability to sense the direction of the underground stream's flow, as well as its presence and depth, though his accuracy as to depth was later questioned by at least one of his clients.

Big Bend ranchers who needed water soon heard of Guy and put him to work. To locate water with his x-ray eyes he witched around Dryden and also for Alpine lawyer Wigfall Van Sickle. The attorney wrote:

That Guy Fenley is possessed of an X-Ray sight cannot be questioned. He has demonstrated his ability to see underground streams of water, no matter what their depth may be, on a number of occasions, and the stockmen of West Texas have ample proof of his power in this line. I engaged him to go to Brewster County and locate two wells on the ranch which is owned by D. J. Combs and myself. This ranch is situated in a very dry country, known as the Glass Mountains. We had made a vain search for water on this ranch, having sunk a well to a depth of 607 feet, at a cost of $1,500, without striking water. This boy has already located two wells on the ranch, one at a depth of 250 feet and the other at a depth of 400 feet, both containing an abundant supply of pure water, and well-drilling outfits are now at work sinking other wells on the ranch, with no doubt about securing water.

There can be no longer any doubt about this boy's wonderful power of sight, for the reason that instances are numerous and notoriously known where his X-Ray gift or whatever it may be called has been proven beyond a doubt. He comes of a splendid family and has fine connections. He is a modest, handsome, blue-eyed boy, and to all outward appearances there is nothing about him to distinguish him from other boys of the same age. While locating the wells in Brewster County he romped and played with other boys whose acquaintance he made. He is bright and intelligent and when in school at Uvalde he stood at the head of his class in mathematics.

I will say that if there is any doubting Thomas, such a person can verify the truth of all my statements concerning the wonderful power of this boy by writing to anyone in Uvalde, Sanderson, or Alpine, Texas. He cannot tell the exact depth of water below the surface, but he approximates its depth as any other person would guess at distances above ground.

A newspaper writer said, "These facts were confirmed by the Honorable John Nance Garner of Uvalde and its representative in the State Legislature." Early in his career Guy refused payment for his services and turned down $500 for locating a water well in Edwards County. His fame, first established in the Big Bend, spread nationwide, and he was overwhelmed with requests to find oil and minerals as well as water.

Early in 1901 the Alpine postmaster received letters from Indiana and Michigan inquiring about Guy Fenley, and lengthy articles about him appeared in newspapers from Seattle to Buffalo. In Austin Representative Garner doubtlessly responded to the request he received about the boy from the Society for Psychical Research in Boston. "We are interested," said Dr. Richard Hodgson, "in accurate accounts from the scientific point of view."

The Boy with the X-ray Eyes provided food for thought on psychical phenomena and earned reference to himself in at least one book on water witching. Then he seems to have dropped from the public's attention almost as suddenly as he had come into it. Harry Hornby, publisher of the Uvalde *Leader-News* says that Fenley settled in Zavala County and lived out a quiet, comfortable life there as district clerk. His early return to obscurity, however, did not leave the Big Bend bereft of water witches.

One of these, John Hackett, was telegraph operator at one of the many little jerkwater Southern Pacific siding stations that now have all but disappeared. Twenty miles southeast of Marathon, Tesnus once had a post office and a population of twenty people. The name of the settlement is Sunset spelled backward, after the SP's Sunset Limited. Sometimes the bleak siding still is used as a shipping point for cattle.

Nobody knew much about Hackett. His black hair, long and thick, grew voluminously down to the seat of his britches. Before losing himself at Tesnus he had been married, but he would not talk about it. Though he did not much avoid women, he had no more to do with them than was necessary. He was thought to be a widower, but nobody really knew whether his wife was dead or the two had split the blanket.

As all that hair persistently got in Hackett's way, he tied black rags around his head and face to control it. He never cut it because, he said, if he did he would lose his power. Therein lay the mysterious force that sustained him in his remarkable efforts.

Hackett's water-finding technique was routine. With the ends of a standard forked limb in his hands, he would walk over the land, his mane lashed down against the wind. His luck in locating productive wells was favorable, and he is remembered also as good at curing a fever.

His simple technique of effecting a cure was to hold the

patient's hand. He was careful to ask how long the patient had been ailing, for this made an important difference in his approach. If a person had run a high fever for only a short time, he would grasp the hand, concentrate with all his might, and throw a mighty jolt of his power into the sufferer. This would take the temperature down to about normal in less than an hour. If, on the other hand, the sick person had run the fever for several days, he proceeded more cautiously, set the brakes on his power, and applied it gently. Hackett said that, if he tried to make such a fever go away too fast, the patient could not stand the full force he would pour into him. It might kill him.

Once a year this recluse and mysogynist set his table for two at an evening meal. Across from an empty chair and empty plate he dined alone, and throughout the supper he would converse with his absent wife. It was believed they caught each other up on their separate doings of the previous twelve months, but nobody ever knew for sure.

Crowding the age of ninety, Alpine rancher Perry Cartwright still is the most sprightly and respected water witch in the Big Bend. He stands about five feet seven and looks as though he might weigh 108 pounds with both pockets full of staples. Gently spoken, blue-eyed, and a wiry, hard worker, he lives alone since his wife's death in their home on the edge of town. There is not a more pleasant, relaxing companion than Perry Cartwright, and I have spent considerable time with him talking about the folk skill he practices.

Tell me, Perry. How do you go about witching?

I use one forked rod and one straight rod. The forked rod is a long piece of heavy copper wire bent double with a couple of twists that make a little loop in the fork end, and I had this long slim canvas bag made to keep them in. I changed from the peach limb to wire because fruit limbs are hard to get in the Big Bend country. Besides that, it's hard anywhere to find a tree-fork with equal size branches, and they always give you an unbalanced pull.

To find water I walk with the forked rod and, when I come to water, it dips. The more water, the stronger and faster the dip. For estimating depth I use my depth rod. It's this straight wire about four feet long. I sit on the ground and hold it straight out in front of me with both hands. The wire bobs once for each foot the water is down. When it measures down to a stream—say at 150 feet—it will wave back and forth. Then it will start bobbing again until it bobs on down to the next stream, if there is one.

They say that a witching rod has to come from a fruit-bearing tree, especially peach or apple. But any wire will work. It's the man, not the stick. Another thing that plays a big part, put your mind on what you want to witch for. It sounds kind of silly, but in my mind I just keep asking the rod, "Where's the water? Where's the water?" It makes you tired to witch, because it does take something out of you. After a long day's witching, sometimes I'm exhausted.

Some people use an insulated forked rod of copper wire to witch for oil. If you're over a pool, the size of the pool can be estimated by the length of time the pool holds the rod bent down. The bigger the pool, the more time it takes for the rod to get over the pull. Over a water pool, it always bobs right back up again.

Have you witched for much of anything besides water?

I've experimented by witching for oil where I know it is and also where I know there isn't any. I get in the car and drive over the country and hold the wire. The wire works just as well in the car as it does out walking around with it. One time Pete Kennedy and me tried to witch for a small airplane that was lost in the mountains and the passengers killed. We didn't go into the mountains with our rods. We stayed home and witched over a map, but we couldn't find it. I think the reason we failed was we both pretty well had our minds made up in advance about where we thought it was. But we were away off.

I've tried for money too. One time near Alpine a girl and her mother were walking along the road from the gate to the house. The girl threw her mother two silver dollars and her mother caught one, but the other fell in the dirt and got covered up and they couldn't find it. A fellow who lived on the place brought me a peach rod with a dime fixed where the fork joined. I hunted around and finally held it over a place in the road where the stick dipped and straightened up. And there was the money.

The wire can be used for mental telepathy too. One time my wife wanted to go see her mother, who lived in Dallas, but we knew she'd been visiting in Georgia.

My wife said, "Perry, get your wire and see if Mother's home. I don't believe she is."

So I got my straight wire and held it out in front of me and asked if my wife's mother was home in Dallas. The wire bobbed up and down for "Yes." (If it sways back and forth sideways, it's "No.") And sure enough, my wife went on to Dallas and her mother was there.

Neighbors of mine, Mr. and Mrs. Leath, had kinfolks in Big Lake with a sick child. Mrs. Leath was worried about it and asked me one day if I'd telephone her folks in Big Lake and check on it.

I said, "If I had my wire, I could tell you."

So I went to my car, got my wire, and checked. I went back and told Mrs. Leath, "They are all well, and they've written you a letter, and your mother will get the letter tomorrow."

Well, Mrs. Leath didn't believe it. I saw her again two days later and asked her if they'd gotten the letter. She was kind of peeved about it and snapped, "Yes! I got a letter yesterday. How did you do that?"

I told her, "With my wire. Mental telepathy."

She walked off and said, "Work of the devil!"

I've heard several stories that claim to be cases of mental telepathy.

There are many instances of it. In Haskell City a doctor was on a call in his buggy one day. It was raining and the creek was up and he couldn't get home, but he decided to cross it anyway. Back home his little girl had gone to play with neighbor children. While she was playing, her daddy was crossing the creek and was about to wash away.

Her daddy thought about his family and said, "I'm gone!"

Right then back home his little girl ran to her mother crying and screaming, "Father's drowning!" She was all upset until finally her daddy did get home. She ran to him and hugged him and was crying with relief.

She picked up his thoughts when he thought he was "gone" and was thinking of his family.

The rod won't work for everybody. I know it won't work for me, because I've tried it. What kind of people does it work for?

My grandfather said only one in a family could do it and that not all families had the one. Some say only a seventh son can do it, but that's not so. A lot of people say it's electricity or radar, but I disagree. It may be mental telepathy.

Whatever it is, it's a gift from God, and that's why I don't make any charge for it. The way I feel about it, if I can help the other fellow, that's repayment enough for me. Sometimes they give me presents. Pete Kennedy gave me two horses that I'm mighty proud of.

Do water witches usually charge a fee?

Courtney Mellard over at Marfa used to charge $50 a location. Some charge $25 a location and a $100 a well if it comes in.

Who are some other water witches you know in the Big Bend?

John Harmon—he's dead now—witched. His brother Sam —he's dead too—was a great believer, but the stick would never do a thing for him. But anybody who thought he could find water, Sam would take him around. He checked me against others and saw that we all found pretty much the same water formations. Luther Yarbro at Ruidoso witched, and Ol Cleveland, and he's not here any more. Luther was one of the best, even though he was crippled up with rheumatism and almost blind. Pete Kennedy witches.

Have there been any other water witches in your family besides yourself?

Yes. Grandfather Cartwright lived in Grayson County. He used a straight stick, usually peach. He witched wells all over that part of the country and could tell the depth to within a foot or closer. That's shallow-well country, and it's easier to locate a well ten to fifty feet than a hundred- to a thousand-foot well, like it is in the Big Bend. There are so many formations in deep-well country like this that it's difficult to estimate the depth. But you can usually tell it.

Grandfather also used his rod to find horses and sheep that had strayed off. During the Civil War he was in the army. My father and father's brother stayed home—they were six and ten years old—and had a little flock of sheep. They got lost and the boys couldn't find them.

Well, that same day Grandfather came back from the army. He took his rod and went behind the barn and soon came back and told the boys, "You go up that little draw to the head of it. Go over the hill and turn to your left. Then go across another hill to the head of another draw, and you'll find the sheep." The boys went just like Grandfather told them, and there were the sheep.

The boys didn't learn much about it from Grandfather. He was killed soon after the war, and he didn't talk much about it anyway, because people said it was the work of the devil.

How did you find out that you could witch for water?

It was like this. Grandfather had a daughter—my aunt— that used the rod. My father moved to Knox City, Texas, and his sister was visiting us one time when I was about twenty-one or twenty-two. We had no water, so she witched around the place and found a stream of water. Three or four of us were talking about it, and one said to me, "Perry, why don't you try it?"

She used a forked peach limb, so I took her limb and tried it, and it worked for me on the same place she found water. A year later a well was drilled there, but the water was salty.

By the time I was twenty-five years old we had built a rent house on the place and we wanted water there, but Father didn't believe there was any. So I witched around by myself and found a stream of water.

After that, Father said, "Perry, if you can find water there, I'll believe you can find it."

So I witched over a clay hill, and the rod dipped right over the water. I said, "The water goes right over here." And sure enough, at sixty-five feet they struck a good well. At this time, though, I didn't yet estimate the depth.

About half a mile away I witched another well. Then about 1912 I left Knox City for Brewster County. Out here I witched for different people and got some wells. Then I got to trying for depth and was right on the majority of them.

Tell me about some of the wells you've witched in the Big Bend.

In years past I witched eleven wells for Jim Logan on his place—all good. A friend of Jim's needed water, and Jim told him, "Get Perry Cartwright and witch that well. He'll find water for you like he did for me. But I had to drill seventeen hundred feet one time to keep him from being a liar."

I've found ten or twelve for Pete Kennedy—all good—and one for Gay Meriwether and two for Ed Davidson. I've found three or four wells for Joe Espy at Fort Davis. I've witched a lot for the Kokernots. Old Man Kokernot [Herbert Kokernot, Sr.] never wanted to drill more than a hundred feet, so some I got for him were dry holes.

I guess my most unusual find was on Mrs. Jim Anderson's place, south of Alpine. I found three wells on that place in 1956. One of those wells comes so close to the surface that they tie a quart can on a sotol stalk and dip water. It comes to within four or five feet of the top of the ground, and sometimes they ditch it into the creek and make the creek run when it's dry.

I knew it would be a good well. The stronger the pull on the stick, the better the well, the more water there is there, and the closer it is to the surface.

Another good well I found was on Limpia Creek on Kokernot's place. They drilled a hundred and seventy to eighty feet and water came within thirty feet of the top.

Have you had any failures?

Well, on the U-Up-and-Down, the McIver ranch, one time I witched two wells. The first one, I estimated the depth at 318 or 320, and we got water at 318. I estimated the other at 350 to 357. We drilled to 360 and there wasn't any water in sight. He kept drilling to see if I was right in saying there was water there at all, and at 740 feet he got a good well. So I missed that one almost 300 feet.

I found water for Willis McCutcheon on Josephine Kokernot's place. He drilled thirteen hundred feet and quit. He hadn't struck water, but it's there. All he has to do is keep on drilling till he strikes it.

I've found twelve or thirteen wells for Richard Merrill

and his father and Richard's wife. I saw Richard at the Bloys
Camp Meeting in the Davis Mountains after that. Richard was
talking to a bunch of men, and when he saw me, told these
other fellows, "Perry witched a well for me and missed the
depth."

That made me feel pretty funny with everybody listening in. Then he said, "Perry said I'd get water at 150 feet, but
I didn't. I didn't get water till I'd drilled 150 feet and four
inches."

Well, that made me feel better.

Has the city of Alpine had any of its wells witched?

In the past nearly all the Alpine city wells were witched.
The city's best wells were witched. Take the one on the South
Hill. Louie Starnes said when he was mayor he was hunting
water. He tried geologists and he tried his own judgment but
wasn't having any luck. Then he asked me to help, and I
found one well that pumps 150 gallons a minute.

I found it on the edge of the stream. Then I witched
around and found the middle of the stream, they drilled, and
in good times that well pumps five hundred gallons a minute.
After the drouth in the 1950s it only pumped two to three
hundred gallons. Other city wells I've located are the one by
the Terlingua Road south of town and two on the Fort Davis
highway north of town.

The city didn't drill those on the Fort Davis road as I
recommended. The one farthest from the road, by the Santa
Fe tracks, is on a kind of whirlpool of a stream. I recommended they drill this one only and not drill the other. By drilling
the other they tapped the only flow this stream has. They'd
get more water if they'd drilled only the one near the tracks.

*What is the water witch's idea of underground forma-
tions? How do you detect them?*

If you find a flowing stream, hold the rod sideways and
the rod will bend in the direction of the flow. If the water is

stationary, the fork of the rod will either remain stationary or go around and around.

Sometimes you find a pool, or dome, of water. I've gotten wells on two or three of these. Say you find a dome with no stream flowing off it. The water comes straight up from below. You can trace the boundary of a dome by watching the dips in the rod.

Sometimes you drill and might drill through three or four strata of water. And the deeper you drill, the better the water, the more there is of it. Some strata have streams flowing away from them. These streams usually make good wells. They give a good supply of water and don't vary.

I've had good luck finding water for everybody but myself. I thought I had a good well on my place one time, and I drilled and got a dry hole. I took Luther Yarbro to my dry hole, and he worked it with his wire and said, "There's lots of water there when you get to it. But it may be a thousand feet." Pete Kennedy says there's water in my dry hole too.

This water is where two streams cross, one over the other. The larger stream comes from a dome a mile and a half away. It's a strong dome. I located one good well on that stream a mile east of the dome and another small well on it. Sometimes you drill in a place where no water is indicated, and water will come into your well from a stream a hundred yards away.

Up in New Mexico one time Pete Kennedy saw a fellow drill 250 or 300 feet and still no water. He was getting desperate. A water witch came along and told him there was no water where he was drilling and then moved him over five feet. He hit water at 125 or 150 feet, and right now a good well and the dry hole are sitting under the same windmill tower.

On Kennedy's place one time I located a stream. Then I found a weak stream that broke off from it. I advised Kennedy to drill on the main stream, and he did and got a good well. The reservoir filled up to about two or three feet and quit. The water was coming from a pool up the country collected about half a mile away.

There are places where depth can't be figured. Most witches say you can't tell the depth, but I'm one of the few that still sticks my neck out.

Geologists might disagree with this concept of underground water in streams with directional flow, pools, and pools with streams flowing off from them.

Maybe they do, but most dowsers have always witched with that in mind, and it works.

Perry Cartwright is not the only water witch who claims credit for some of the wells of Alpine. Bill Gardner, now a gospel singer living in Rincon, New Mexico, says,

> As you are probably aware, I am the man responsible for the discovery of the good water well on the hillside above the old Miles homesite northwest of Alpine in Sunny Glen. The theory that water had to be there was determined by good country-boy logic. But the actual location was determined by the use of a branch from an apple tree that was growing in the flat below the mountain slope to the south of the homesite. I believe that the Alpine *Avalanche* article in 1959 reported it to be a peach branch, but that was an error. The information can be checked with Dr. W. E. Lockhart, as he was mayor of Alpine at that time. I'm sure that he will tell you that some of the city water people questioned my well-being while the well was being drilled there on the side of the mountain in what seemed to be solid rock. But as is past history, the City of Alpine did purchase water rights on that property.

Ardently skeptical of water witching, former mayor Lockhart said, "He got a pretty good well. I'm not going to deny that." The doctor went on to say that "country-boy logic" told Gardner to drill near the growth of trees in a mountainside run-off, that his hitting a water-bearing formation was sheer luck, and that the apple switch had nothing to do with it.

Now witching sometimes works at hydrology's elbow. In

April, 1976, the City of Alpine was about to drill a new water well in Sunny Glen. Several other wells nearby (except the Gardner well) had been located by hydrological methods. These predict a better than fair chance of striking ample water if a hole is drilled with a cable-tool rig in or near a canyon in proper relationship to a towering igneous upthrust that has broken up the horizotonal strata underground, enabling them to carry water that seeps into the earth of a large catchment area, the only source of this water being rainfall. A cable-tool rig must be used, because a rotary rig shuts off the water it bores into by plugging up the layers of broken strata with mud from interspersing layers of clay. Because other wells in Sunny Glen are good producers, it was decided to drill there. Science had spoken. Then came the water witches.

Joking over their coffee, City Manager Bob Stevens and some of the fellows got to talking about witching for the best spot to drill one ten-inch hole in a pasture that could accommodate several football fields. For the fun of it, Stevens called on three water witches, Christmas Mountains rancher Tony Hess, Perry Cartwright, and an anonymous third. First Perry witched around, got a strong dip, held his rod sideways to get the direction of flow, then with his depth rod judged the water to be about 180 feet down. With no knowledge of Perry's location, Tony Hess tried, and his rod pulled less than four feet from the same spot. The third water witch got his reaction about twenty-five feet away. Then Bob Stevens wanted to try it. He took the rod, walked around, and much to his surprise the rod struggled to work for him. He could feel it moving in his hands, not with the vigor it exerted for the other men, but definitely working. Laughing about it he said, "I don't believe in it, you understand, but it sure makes you wonder. The thing about it, though, it was a lot of fun." When Dr. Lockhart heard Bob tell all this, he launched into a fervent antiwitching lecture; nonetheless, he could not prevent the location of the prospective Alpine city well from being the result of a collusion of science and folk ritual.

The rite of water witching is especially popular among water seekers in the Big Bend, for here even the best geologists declare their predictions to be undependable, because of the irregularity of underground structures. In the desperate search for water, science alone is not enough, and witching is resorted to as a means of bolstering confidence before taking the expensive risk of drilling. If a well is a failure, there is some comfort in knowing that nothing was left untried. Sometimes the water witch is called upon before the geologist, his method thought to be of equal or superior reliability. The impulse to invoke mysterious power to locate a well becomes great in a Big Bend rancher with stock to water or in the city fathers of a West Texas town with the water needs of its people to serve. Whether or not the witching rod really finds water, the rod does dip. There seems to be something to it.

6.
The Steer Branded
MURDER

ONE of the strangest tales of the Big Bend tells of a maverick with MURDER branded on its side.

The story begins on a cold, dust-blowing day with several local cattlemen working a roundup on the tan grass flat about thirty miles east of Fort Davis. Leader—or committee chairman—of the roundup was Eugene Kelley, and present was Henry Powe (pronounced "Poe"), soon to lie dead with several bullets in him. He wore a full back beard and had lost his left arm at the elbow in service of the Confederacy. He had come from Alabama to Texas in 1870 and had had some college education. By 1883 he was grazing cattle on public land around Mount Locke, and he helped found the Methodist Church in Alpine. Two other men involved in the shoot-out were Finus ("Fine") Gilliland and Manning ("Mannie") Clements, both of stormy reputation.

Just why Mannie was at the roundup is not clear. Perhaps he was cowboying for one of the owners, or maybe he was hanging around with nothing else to do. Son of a trail boss, he seems to have ridden the Chisholm Trail and was said to have shot two cowboys in the Indian Territory during a cattle drive. His violent family saga says that his father, while candidate for sheriff, was shot to death in Ballinger by the city marshal, this act eventuating in the marshal's having an arm shot off by Mannie's brother-in-law Jim Miller.

Mannie was said to be kin also to John Wesley Hardin, a

cousin. Once Mannie, Hardin, and Jim Miller posed a solid front in Mannie's defense. Somebody had blasted both barrels of a shotgun through the window into an Alpine saloon where a poker game was going on, thereby "spoiling"—as three accounts tell it in the Western mode of understatement—not only one of the players, but his Dead Man's Hand of aces and eights. When Mannie was indicted for the murder, the three kinsmen decided to pay a visit to lawyer Wigfall Van Sickle in Alpine. They walked unannounced into his office and glared at him grimly. Having studied law in the penitentiary, Hardin was now a member of the bar. He stood slapping a copy of the indictment against Mannie across the palm of a hand and said that he had heard that Van Sickle knew of a witness who claimed to have seen Mannie fire that shotgun. Frightened to his toenails, Van Sickle assured the beady-eyed men that it was only rumor. Hardin said he was glad to hear that, and the phalanx of gunslingers departed. The case of Manning Clements never came to trial. Later he served as deputy sheriff, first in Pecos and later in El Paso, where he was killed in 1908 at the Coney Island Saloon.

Little is known about Fine Gilliland. It is for him that Gilliland Canyon in the Glass Mountains near Marathon is named, because that is where he died. Fine was remembered in the Balmorhea area as a small man with a dark complexion and a mean temper. He never married, and he had kin in Snyder. At the fatal roundup Fine was present as an observer for the large cattle company of Dubois and Wentworth, on whose land the roundup was gathered. His range boss wanted him to make sure these small-time ranchers did not claim or alter the brands of cattle not theirs. The sorting-out of stock and their assignment to various owners had begun when Fine rode up.

Forty years later the son Robert Powe wrote his eye-witness account of what happened for Barry Scobee, the Fort Davis chronicler who spent years putting together the Murder Steer story. Robert Powe said:

On January 28, 1891, there was a roundup operating at Leoncita given by the small cattle owners of that country for the purpose of branding calves that had been missed in the fall roundup. Eugene Kelley was in charge of the work. There were two or three thousand cattle in the herd, and among the herd was a brindle bull yearling, unbranded, but [it] wasn't with its mother.

Gene Kelley and Frank Rooney came to Father and told him that the brindle bull belonged to an HHP cow, which was Father's brand. Father asked them if they were positive that the calf (the brindle bull) belonged to his cow; Kelly said he was positive and could swear to it.

Separating cows with unbranded calves began, and Kelley told me to hold the cut. There had been only a few head cut out when the brindle bull came to the edge of the herd, and Father cut it out and then rode back to the herd.

Gilliland came to where I was and asked me if the calf had a mother in the cut. I told him it didn't but that Kelley had told Father that it belonged to an HHP cow. He (Gilliland) said he (Father) would play hell getting it unless he produced the cow, and I rode in and cut it back to the roundup. The yearling passed Father as it went into the herd, and he looked back and saw Gilliland was driving it, so he rode out and met him, and I wasn't close enough to hear what was said.

Father then rode to where Kelley was and apparently talked to him a few seconds, I suppose in regard to his certainty that the calf belonged to Father's cow. Then Father rode into the herd and started to drive the bull out.

Gilliland went to where Father was in the middle of the roundup. They stopped there together a few seconds, and Father then rode to the far side of the roundup and stopped there with Mannie Clements. I saw Father reach into the saddle pocket and knew what that meant, for I knew Manning always carried his pistol in his saddle pocket.

Father went back to the roundup and drove the bull out toward the cut. Gilliland came in a run and tried to drive the bull back into the herd. Gilliland stopped and unbuckled his saddle pocket where he, too, carried a pistol. He took his rope down and overtook the bull and tried to rope it but missed.

Father then shot at the bull. At this time, Gilliland had dropped in behind Father, had gotten off his horse and was squatted down on one knee with his pistol in both hands aiming at Father's back.

I yelled at Father to look out, that Gilliland was going to shoot; by that time he had fired directly at Father's back; Father started to get off his horse and Gilliland shot again. By this time Father was off his horse, and being a one-armed man had to wrap the bridle reins around his arm, the horse (Raleigh) being afraid of the shooting and trying to get away and came near jerking Father down.

In the meantime Gilliland ran up to within five or six yards of Father, and by that time Father had straightened up, facing Gilliland, and they both shot at almost the same time, then both shot again. Father's gun was empty then, for there were only three cartridges in it. Gilliland grabbed Father's pistol and shot him again. Father staggered a few steps and fell on his face dead.

I was so excited I hardly knew what was going on, but I heard someone say, "For God's sake, don't kill that boy!" and on looking up I saw it was Manning Clements. Gilliland had two pistols in his hands. He told Manning to give him a horse and left at a run. I then started for Alpine to notify the Rangers.

I was told some of the cowboys branded the brindle bull as follows: MURDER on one side and JAN 28 91 on the other side.

If they did so, the animal was spared castration, which is a routine operation upon branding. Newt Gourley of Alpine said, "I have seen the little bull a lot of times," and Robert Powe referred to it about five years after the event as "the noted bull." Even though Jesse Pruitt wrote that he had seen the "murder steer" several times, that is but one observation against two by cattlemen who meant "bull" when they said it.

Justice of course was served. Fine Gilliland hid out in the Glass Mountains. Upon Robert Powe's request, Sheriff John B. Gillett of Brewster County started a search and notified lawmen in nearby counties. In a snowfall on January 31, Deputy Sheriff Thalis Cook and Texas Ranger Jim Putman rode into the mountains. As they walked their horses up a canyon, they met a stranger, also on horseback. Cook asked him if he was Fine Gilliland. The stranger responded with two shots, one shattering Cook's kneecap, the other killing his horse. Gilliland spurred his horse in an escape run; Putman dismounted and with his rifle shot Gilliland's horse from under him. Putman ordered Gilliland to surrender only to be shot at from behind the fallen horse. The next time Putman saw enough hat to suit him rise from behind the horse, he blew off the top of Fine Gilliland's head.

Somehow Putman got the wounded Cook into Marathon, part of the way by hack. Shortly afterward in Alpine, a doctor visiting there without his instruments unsuccessfully tried to remove the bullet, using a brace and bit borrowed from a blacksmith shop. Gilliland's body was brought into Alpine, where kinsmen met it and took it to Snyder. Henry Powe, the man he killed, was buried in Alpine out of the Methodist Church.

As talk about the event flourished, the legend of The Steer Branded MURDER took form. It captured the imagination of Judge Van Sickle, whose wife good humoredly told of his trying hard to promote it as a regular legend. Instinctively classing the little bull as a pariah, he told Scobee, "It became an outcast from its kind. Now and then a cowboy riding home in the dusk from a long day's work would glimpse it on a skyline against the sunset glow, or silhouetted on the rising moon. Then, at the sight or sound of the rider, it would vanish, fleeing away in the obscurity of night as if ashamed to be seen— as if it feared and hated mankind. Like the Wandering Jew of ancient tradition, it seemed to be condemned to roam the earth forever without the surcease of death."

Some say the Murder Steer's hair all turned gray, and some say it was only the hair that haired over the brands, which left them still legible. At the old saloon in Alpine, after each of several killings that took place during arguments over the murder of Powe or over the death of Gilliland, the steer reportedly stuck his head in the window and cut loose with a blood-clabbering bawl. They say also that the maverick, like an agent of evil, appears nearby when any murder at all occurs in the Big Bend and disappears before he can be roped.

Probably the first written account of the Murder Steer was that by Van Sickle for the Galveston *News* in about 1896. Having heard the tale from the lawyer, Barry Scobee fiction-ized it for *Adventure Magazine*, April, 1919. Soon afterward Tex O'Reilley, inventor of Pecos Bill, told Scobee, "You beat me to it. I was just about to write that yarn myself." Scobee wrote it again for *The Cattleman*, March, 1936, and there have since been numerous retellings in publications like *True West* and *Frontier Times*.

It is not the killing that makes the story. Such killings are commonplace enough in western lore. What fastens on the imagination is the branding of MURDER on that brindled bull and turning him loose a herdless animal.

Of the four men known to have put themselves on record as having seen the bull, only Van Sickle said he saw the brand, and Scobee established that the lawyer simply fabricated his entire story. What Van Sickle told Mrs. Jack Shipman of Mar-fa in 1933 seems to be about what he wrote for the Galveston paper. When he was district attorney, he said, he was riding from Alpine to court in Fort Stockton. As he told it:

> In those days the judge and the district attorney went on horseback with their lassos and their running irons in the sad-dle. When more than halfway to Fort Stockton, I discovered a lonely red yearling on the hillside and requested the judge to wait a moment, saying we would start a Maverick brand, and the first throw of my lasso roped the yearling and threw him down on his right side and I motioned the judge to come up.
>
> In the meantime I had started a fire to heat the running iron and when the judge approached he made the remark that brands were usually put on the left side. Thereupon he lassoed the yearling by his hind legs and turned him with his left side up, and, behold! A brand was disclosed. It was "Murder" in letters extended from the jaw to the tail. After some consulta-tion the little red bull was released.

It does not appear that Van Sickle invented the branding episode, though he had a considerable hand in the proliferation of this legend. His invented description of the brand has been carried on by illustrators who have portrayed a steer with letters a foot high all over his ribs. Such a drawing by Tom Lea appears in J. Frank Dobie's *The Longhorns.*

After the killing, the cowboys performed at least one ritual in obedience to human urges and stresses as primeval as the story of Cain. They built a cairn of stones where Henry Powe fell, on the ground that drank his blood. Such stones are piled where blood is spilled or to cover a corpse in order to quiet the troublesome spirit that otherwise might rise up to call down inflictions from supernatural powers, as did Abel's blood upon Cain. The Lord said, "The voice of thy brother's blood crieth unto me from the ground. And now art thou cursed from the earth, which has opened her mouth to receive thy brother's blood." The cairn also is a monument and a memorial to mark the place where some event occurred that is at least of legendary, if not epic, proportion. Ben Pruett of Marfa said, "J. B. Irving showed me one time the mound of rocks where Mr. Powe was shot down by Fine Gilliland."

Whatever those cowboys did or did not do in shock reaction after the killing on that cold and windy day, the legend ritualizes in some detail a set of collective subconscious predispositions at least as ancient as the domestication of cattle. The Lord told Moses, "The goat on which the lot fell to be the scapegoat shall be presented before the Lord to make an atonement with him [for the sins of the people] and to let him go for a scapegoat into the wilderness." The biblical scapegoat ritual was much more complicated than that ascribed to the Big Bend cowboys, but both what those cowboys did and what they are said to have done was enough to vitalize Carl Jung's theory that cultural memories remain in the depths of the mind.

Those disturbed cattlemen were reacting in thoughtless, emotional upheaval. They were deeply involved in shock, rage, grief, despair, and quandary. What they did—or what the legend says they did—can be seen as an intuitive adaptation of their customary occupational folkways to unconsciously recalled ritual. The function of their ritual was first to restore order and expunge guilt, then, according to the legend, to elect and stigmatize a scapegoat which would carry away forever the evil forces that had brought chaos to their well-ordered existence.

The roundup was a cluster of occupational folkways controlling the social, moral, and economic order of cattle raising for profit on the range. On a fateful day these men were placidly performing those ceremonies in the customary manner—cutting properly branded cattle from the roundup into the rightful owner's cut, branding and castrating bull calves that were with their branded mothers, agreeing upon the ownership of motherless calves or mavericks, then branding and castrating them also. By custom, the roundup leader made the final decision if a question of ownership arose. These customs fulfill the economic order—the brand as proof of ownership, emasculation to put more weight on the steer and increase his value. As part of the rite the cowboy eats the calf testicles roasted at the branding-iron fire, then jokes about how good they are and how much they will stimulate his virility. The roundup is a jovial, cooperative, hard-working, economic and social function, its unwritten rules of order plainly and mutually understood.

This particular roundup was horribly jolted out of its routine with the late arrival of a small, dark man who imposed judgment over that of the leader. This godlike being intruded his alien force into the system. By sanction of the leader the unbranded yearling belonged to Henry Powe. Order began to fall apart when the intruder disputed that judgment, and, when the shooting started, it was destroyed.

What was the cause? The brindled bull. If that yearling had not been there, nothing unusual would have happened. Upon his head was laid the guilt, and a ceremonial to transfer that guilt, if not actually performed, has been performed imaginatively in the formation of the legend.

The story says that, first, the cowboys stigmatized the bull in a way so that it would never belong to anybody. Whoever would claim an animal marked MURDER? It was outcast because it was the agent to man of what Wayland Hand calls "imponderable forces that lie behind the visible universe, awakening in him not only feelings of awe, but those of fear as well"—or "fear of the gods," what the Greeks called *deisidaimonia* and what we call "superstition." Not even the maverick hunter with the longest rope would gather this marked pariah into his questionable herd.

Second, by not castrating the bull, the cowboys fully insured the casting-out of the Murder animal. The scapegoat remained a bull, not useful and not wanted in the cattle business. Having disrupted order, this creature was unclean and unfit to be used for food. He was not to be fattened for sale or for the table. In the world of the cattleman he was tabu.

The story goes that those men were still not fully settled in spirit. A final act of some kind was needed to conclude the matter and to bring reassurance that order was indeed restored. They finalized their series of atonement-occupational rites by rolling the little bull over for one more branding. On his unmarked side they burned JAN 28 91. After that date, life as usual could resume. Order, having been disrupted by the malice of unknown powers, was restored.

What finally became of the Murder Bull scapegoat? In 1935 Robert Powe said, "I suppose I am the only person living that knows what became of the noted bull. There was a man by the name of Bill Allen driving a trail herd to Montana. [This was in about 1896.] I asked him if he would take the animal out of the country. He said he would, and I got him to put it in the herd and I went with it to the Pecos River at Horse Head Crossing—that is where they crossed the river and that is the last I ever saw of the brindle bull."

"And Aaron shall lay both his hands upon the head of the

live goat and confess over him all the iniquities of Israel and all their transgressions in all their sins, putting them upon the head of the goat and shall send him away by the hand of a fit man into the wilderness."

7.
Indian Emily and Dolores

INSIDE the grounds of old Fort Davis stands a gravestone which doubles as a historical marker over a burial identified as Indian Emily. South of town is a low, flat-topped hill with a gentle ascent known as Dolores Mountain. Indian Emily is said to have died for love, Dolores reputedly lived for it, and both women became the subjects of local legends.

In the Anglo-American "Lover's Leap" tradition of sentimental Indian legends, the Indian Emily motif has attached itself to several old army posts throughout the United States. Before 1919 Carlysle Graham Raht heard the story in Fort Davis, and it was told to him also in El Paso by the former lieutenant Henry O. Flipper, the black West Pointer who served at Fort Davis until 1882, when he was discharged there because of racial prejudice against him. Giving the story its first printed form in 1919, Raht said:

> After the re-occupation of Fort Davis in 1867, the little settlement, located as it was in the heart of the Apache country, stood the brunt of the Indian attacks. One morning, the inhabitants were awakened by the war-whoop, as the Apaches poured into the outskirts of the town from the nearby hills and canyons. The surprise was complete; but aided by the presence of several large freight outfits which had camped in Fort Davis on their way over the Chihuahua Trail, the soldiers and citizens managed to beat off the attack and inflict severe punishment on the marauders. Many dead and wounded Indians were left on the ground. Among the latter was a young Indian girl. She was badly wounded, and would have been taken to

the hospital with the other wounded had not a Mrs. Easton insisted on taking care of her. Mrs. Easton finally nursed the young squaw back to health, and kept her for a companion and servant.

For two years, Emily, as the girl was named, lived with the Easton family. She had grown accustomed to the ways of the whites, and her stay among them seemed indefinite. Mrs. Easton's son, Lieutenant Thomas Easton, was a great favorite with Emily, and in a shy, unobtrusive way, she attended his wants.

Then the Nelsons moved to Fort Davis. Immediately, Thomas Easton was attracted to Mary Nelson, an occurrence which did not escape the keen eyes of the Indian girl. She began to act queerly, and for hours at a time, she would sit and gaze at the mountains, as though she was considering some action of which she was uncertain. The day the engagement of Tom and Mary was announced, Emily disappeared.

For some time, Mrs. Easton hoped for Emily's return, but the months stretched into a year, with no word of the girl. The newly acquired daughter, however, made up for the loss of Emily; but the Indian girl was not forgotten.

The Apaches had become more troublesome than usual; raids were more frequent and increased in boldness. The soldiers were kept busy and the post command was constantly on the lookout for an attack on Fort Davis. One night, during this troublesome time, a sentry heard someone trying to pass him. Suspecting it might be an Indian, he called, "Halt, or I fire!" Instead of making reply, the intruder broke into a run towards the post buildings. The sentry took careful aim and fired. The shot was answered by a scream in a feminine voice. The soldier rushed up to the fallen woman, who proved to be an Indian squaw, and lifting her carefully in his arms, he carried her to the commanding officer's quarters. It was Emily, and and she was mortally wounded.

Mrs. Easton was immediately sent for. Upon seeing her friend, Emily, with failing breath, gasped out: "All my people come to kill—I hear talk—by light of morning—maybe you know—Tom no get killed—good-bye"—and the faithful Indian girl was gone. The Indians did come, and in a force sufficient to annihilate the unprepared settlement; but Emily's warning had been in time to make preparation, and the Indians were beaten back with heavy losses.

The next two printed versions of Raht's Indian Emily story, both by the same man, are somewhat different. Barry Scobee's 1947 account carries on the sentimental tradition, but in his 1963 version he places a high value on historical veracity with its tendency to subject legend to rational and documentary tests. The American reader and tale teller, growing skeptical of the earlier "Lover's Leap" sentiment, preferred facts instead.

In the first edition of *Old\Fort Davis* it suited Scobee's purpose to emphasize that "Emily was in love with Tom," that "Mrs. Easton was fond of Emily," and that Emily was a "beautiful Indian girl." He created a sentimental southern slave-master relationship. When Emily was captured, Mrs. Easton "put her in the adobe hut behind their house in Officer's Row" and "Emily stayed on as a maid and companion to Mrs. Easton." This relationship was barely suggested in Raht, but Scobee's Emily always keeps in her place. When shot, "she called for Mrs. Easton"—not for the married man she loves—and it is to his mother that she delivers the warning: "I tell you so Tom no get killed."

Yet Scobee's first version anticipates his more objective second when he adds a few historical facts. He tells of how Emily's grave was once marked with a board that read, "Indian Squaw—Killed by Accident." He says he was present when the stone-covered burial place was located for the Texas State Centennial Commission so that the present marker might be erected. It reads:

HERE LIES INDIAN EMILY
AN APACHE GIRL
WHOSE LOVE FOR A
YOUNG OFFICER INDUCED
HER TO GIVE WARNING OF
AN INDIAN ATTACK.
MISTAKEN FOR AN ENEMY
SHE WAS SHOT BY A

SENTRY, BUT SAVED THE
GARRISON FROM MASSACRE

ERECTED BY THE STATE OF TEXAS
1936

After fifteen years Scobee rewrote the story in *Fort Davis Texas, 1583–1960*. He now had access to Fort Davis documents and microfilm, and the newer book carries more of history and less of legendry than the older. In it Scobee desentimentalizes the Indian Emily story, reduces it to one paragraph, and gives several new papagraphs of evidence and analysis. He makes clear that "there is no evidence that Indians ever attacked the fort," whereas in the legend they attack the fort twice.

Yet he still seems to be searching for some factual basis to the story when he cites an 1868 report that an "Indian female child" was brought to Fort Davis by soldiers after a skirmish with Apaches in the Dead Horse Mountains. Coincidentally or not, the date of 1868 matches the approximate dating by Raht of the girl's capture. Scobee goes on to conjecture that Emily was killed during the height of Indian activity, about 1880. He establishes beyond doubt that the grave was once marked by a board inscribed "Indian Squaw—Killed by Accident."

Skeptical historians discredit the story out of hand. For instance, Frank Smith, distinguished historian of the Army in the West and first superintendent of the Fort Davis National Historical Site, snorted and scoffed at the Indian Emily tale and told me it must have been lifted right out of a Harold Bell Wright novel. It was not malice toward folklore, however, but considerations of accurate restoration that led to closing the ruts leading to the Indian Emily grave, thus separating it about a quarter mile from the main roads in the old fort. (This separation has prompted outcries from tourists who arrive there bent on visiting Indian Emily's grave immediately, and at least one impassioned speech, delivered by State Rep-

resentative Gene Hendryx to the Alpine Rotary Club, demanded that the United States government give the people
easier access to the legendary burial.)

Some trained historians, rummaging among Fort Davis
documents for other data, have come across items that seem
related somehow to the ephemeral Indian Emily. They have
pointed out that when Fort Davis was deactivated in 1891,
the post cemetery was moved to San Antonio, with the exception of one grave, "Indian Squaw." Bruce Lamberson ran
across a post surgeon's report of January, 1882: "A cowardly
and brutal murder of an Indian captive (squaw) was perpe-
trated by some party or parties unknown near the Hospital
where the woman was tented. The deed was done with an
axe or some other sharp instrument—her head being split
open, and rape seems to have been the object."

As for other characters in the legend, Lamberson leafed
through the army register to discover that before 1900 there
was never an army officer of any rank by the name of Easton.
He found that in 1871 there was at Fort Davis a civilian clerk
called Mr. Easton, and in an old San Antonio newspaper article he noticed reference to a Mr. Easdon at Fort Davis, a
mechanic. Lieutenant Easton was supposed to have married
into a family of Nelsons, but Lamberson stumbled upon only
a Mr. Nelson, who witnessed a murder in the little town.

Thus the objective, historical mind gives strength to the
legendary properties of the story by turning up facts that
hasten its death as history. Perhaps the most important aspect
of the historian's compulsive interest, however, is that even
he is captured by the spell that the old yarn casts upon the
imagination.

So the legend lives on in both oral and written traditions.
In *The Big Bend Country of Texas* Virginia Madison uses
restraint by desentimentalizing the language of her narrative
and letting emotional appeal crop out as it will from the story
itself. She preserves the detail, found in all three previous
book versions, of Emily's running away to her people on the

very day of the announcement of Tom's engagement to Mary. Louise Cheney, who wrote up the tale for *The West* magazine, invented dialogue and details expected by such publications. A spinoff versified account is that by Faye Carr Adams, called "Em'ly, the Chieftain's Daughter." In it Emily has been promoted to the rank of Indian Princess, appropriate to the "Lover's Leap" tradition. To intensify the drama, when Emily is shot,

> The sentry called and who should come
> But the captain she loved so dear,
> He lifted her and called her name—
> And then death held no fear.

Folklorists and historians may scoff at the sentimental, pseudo Indian legends that have attached themselves to so many cliffs and old army posts throughout this land. Such stories should be regarded as what they are, genuine folk expressions of American urban folk. Indian Emily makes a good story, sentimentalism and all.

In another Fort Davis legend, the romantic Mexican characters are a beautiful, innocent señorita and a simple, honest, serape-clad young peasant. The story of Dolores is based on some confirmed facts. Dolores Gavino Doporto was the actual personage, said to be demented, who periodically lighted fires at night on a mesa near Fort Davis, a promontory called Dolores Mountain. She died in 1893, probably in her fifties if Major W. H. Clapp's figures can be relied upon. They say she was burning her signal fire in an effort to make contact with her lover, José, who was killed by Indians on the eve of their unfulfilled wedding day. This story harks back further than the Indian Emily tale, to about a year or two after the fort was founded in 1854.

The earliest version is a poem written by Major Clapp in 1885 to be recited at a party on the post by Mrs. Belle Marshall Locke, a rancher's wife and former actress. The genteel function the poem was to serve helps account for Barry Scobee's judgment that it "may win no awards for rhythm or meter, but certainly it should for sentiment." Considering the social event it was to serve, the poem's opening, in which Major Clapp curiously combines West Texas local color with his book learning about ancient Egypt, should come as no surprise. He then classes the frontier settler as a ruffian, just as James Fenimore Cooper had classed Ishmael Bush in *The Prairie*. When the poet gets to the main characters, Dolores is the beautiful, rustic señorita, and José is a dashing caballero, a scout for the U. S. Army and a good tracker experienced in shooting dangerous Indians. It is a rather long poem, it is not a dull one, and it abounds with feelings typical of the sentimental local legend.

Dolores

by Major W. H. Clapp

Beside a Post, on the far frontier
Has grown up a village, quaint and queer;
In its straggling rows of mud jacals
With flat earth roofs, where the Mexican dwells,
Where the sun-dried bricks are the same today
As those that were made of Egyptian clay
By the weary Israelite long ago,
And piled with labour near the flow
Of the patient Nile; and even their name
Remains—as then—forever the same.
Adobes still—although the name
Has been carried across the sea to Spain;
Then far to the land of the Aztec where
The soldiers and monks built missions fair.
Mummied old word it seems to be,
Coming so far across the sea,
Picturing now as it pictured then,
The rude endeavors of barbarous men.
In this frontier village in the far Southwest,
With its mud-walled homes, where even the best
Are meager and poor, lives a motley crew
Of Mexicans, Negroes, and a few

Frontier Americans here and there,
The ne'er-do-wells of a race more fair.

In one poor hovel there dwells alone
A withered old woman whose face has grown
Haggard and yellow; her hair is grey,
And her journey through life a weary way.
Her eyes to the future seem to cling,
As though waiting, alas! for some distant thing
That is long in coming; and yet, 'tis said,
She was beautiful once and soon to wed,
That her step was agile and full of grace,
Her laugh, sweet music; and in her face
Was the charm of youth, with never a trace
Of sorrow or care—the pride of her race.
Dolores, they called her, and failed to see
In this sorrowful name a prophecy.

Her lover was manly and strong of limb;
He knew the trails in the mountains grim
And his rifle was never known to fail,
Or his sight grow dim when on the trail
Of the thieving Indian who lurked around
And murdered and scalped whenever he found
An unarmed party, or one too slow.
But this was thirty long years ago.
Thirty long years since one autumn day
José, with his rifle and mustang grey,
Stopped at the door goodbye to say
To gentle Dolores, that fatal day.
Her eyes grew dim, and in gentle tones
She besought her lover with tears and groans
To abandon the journey. Alas! that he
Had not her vision somewhere to see
In heeded omen the fearful fate
Which he dared that day, and e'er too late
Take note of the pain in her warning eyes
And interpret aright her heart's sad sighs.
What is that power to the loving given
Sometimes to see from their fond hearts riven
The cherished form that is far away,

Compelling a sigh when others are gay?
Or to feel, when danger is near,
The shuddering touch of a nameless fear?
A voiceless feeling, a speechless dread,
Like the sigh of a soul to a dead soul wed?
A few there are to whom it speaks
In unsyllabled words, and ever seeks
To carry a warning, with spirit breath,
And hinder the icy hand of death.

José rode off with a last goodbye
And hardly noticed the sorrowful sigh
That parted the lips of Dolores; then
Turned his mustang's head to the rocky glen
Of the Musquiz Canyon, famed alway
For its fatal deed in Indian fray.
She watched; he came not. The second day,
A goatherd, following the stony way
That led to the canyon, found him dead
Where his mustang fell in the rocky bed.
He was pierced with arrows and scalped, alas!
While near at hand the trampled grass
Showed where an Indian ambuscade
Had lain and watched and finally made
An end of his life. There is nothing strange
In an end like this for those who range
The western border and scout the plain,
For many have never come back again;
Nor that to those who have lovers and friends
There ever is sorrow when strong life ends,
And ever a moan for a life that is done
For each unknown man is somebody's son.
All that remained of poor José
Was carried back to the Fort that day
And kindly buried; but with it lay
The heart of Dolores. Not a ray
Of hope remained. She had no moan,
Nor shed a tear, but sadly, alone
With downcast eye and sigh of pain,
She took up life's irksome cares again.
She did such duties as near her lay,
Yet never again from that fatal day

Was seen to smile; and her widowed heart
Lived henceforth from the world apart;
While ever her sad voice seemed to be
Sweet as some far-off minstrelsy.
More than fifteen-hundred times since then
She has wended her way up the flinty glen,
And high above yon torrent's bed
Has kindled a flame to her long lost dead.
Once each week when the darkness falls,
With a reverent love that never palls,
With trembling footsteps and tear-stained cheek
She goes to the mountain there to seek
In the fitful flame, perchance to find
The face of her lover, or to hear in the wind
The sound of his voice. The night may be wet
And bitter, and cold. And even yet
When the norther's breath in an hour or less
Chills with its shivering, wild caress
The heart of its victim, she goes the same,
Heedless of weather or weary frame,
And kindles anew in the silent night
The flickering flame of her beacon light;
Watches it brighten, then fade and die;
Then homeward turns with a weary sigh.

Think of it, ye who mourn today,
Who beside the graves of your dead still pray,
Who doff your mourning in one short year,
And forget, in that time, the tear-stained bier
Of those you lost; then remember, please,
How patient and faithful, on bended knees,
Dolores mourned in the far Southwest;
Then say, if you will, who loved the best.

Mrs. Locke, for whom the poem was written, was not
the only one who saw the fires many times burning for hours
on the mountain at night in all kinds of weather. In the fall
of 1893, as a guest at the ranch of General B. H. Grierson,
Mrs. Locke called attention to the blaze, and the general replied, "It's only the crazy old Mexican woman with her fire

for her dead lover." A few days later the general reported to his guest, "Well, the old woman Dolores will build no more fires for José. She is dead." Though the grave of Dolores has not been identified, she is supposedly buried in a Fort Davis cemetery. Remembering the event from his childhood, Roy Bloys of Fort Davis heard that she came to her end in agony, having purposely poisoned herself with an herb tea of her own making.

The variations in Barry Scobee's 1947 version of the Dolores story clearly arise from oral sources and not from the poem. In dressing up the oral versions for print, Scobee does not diminish the charm of the girl, but José is demoted to goatherd, with no trace of the poetic caballero. In this later account the story has accumulated dramatic elements not present in the poem: the couple had already the habit of signaling each other with fires and, while José is gone on his last herding camp, Dolores makes preparations for their wedding upon his return. In the more recent version Dolores goes insane, whereas Major Clapp attributed her weekly fires to her undying love and devotion. Here is Scobee's account, based on tales he heard:

> Dolores was beautiful, with soft, appealing brown eyes like those of a young doe wounded unto death; and no princess ever carried herself with statelier grace than this lowly Mexican girl who dwelt in the dingy little settlement of "Chihuahua" on the outskirts of the town of Fort Davis.
>
> José, the goatherd, was her sweetheart, and he tended his flock on the side of the mountain a few miles from town. Sometimes he would be gone for days at a time with the flock, and he and Dolores had agreed that during his absence each would, from time to time, light a signal fire as an assurance of their love and fidelity. Dolores would build her fire on the low flat mountain just south of town, and José would build his on some peak near his flock.
>
> The wedding day had been set, the little adobe house which was to be their home had been built and the rude furnishings placed therein. With patient fingers Dolores had taken the last stitch in her simple wedding gown, and all the young people

in the Mexican settlement were eagerly awaiting the wedding. But it was not to be.

One day, as José was watching his flocks in a rocky glen near Musquiz Canyon, the Indians came and killed and scalped him. When he did not return home, a search party went out and found his body, and, instead of a marriage, there was a funeral. Dolores, yesterday a bright-eyed laughing girl, now looked into the face of her dead lover with burning tearless eyes and followed his body to the grave with listless step, like a ghost "doomed for a certain time" to walk the earth.

None of the homely duties she was wont to perform in her father's house was neglected, but thereafter every Thursday night, with a bundle of fagots over her shoulder, she crept away from the merry crowd who gathered in the little settlement to talk and laugh and sing Spanish love songs, and went up the mountain to light a fire and commune with her dead.

The Anglo-American versions of the Dolores and Indian Emily stories have made their way from oral tradition into printed versions by flowery writers, thence back into oral tradition again in more simplified forms. A literate society transmits many of its folk tales in that way. Whatever basic facts these legends may have sprung from, those facts have been augmented by the sentimental imagination in the American manner. Indian Emily seems to be a fictitious, traveling anecdote that was connected as pseudo local history to several localities. While the Dolores story has considerable factual foundation, it too has accumulated sentiment and dramatic coincidence.

Among Mexican-Americans of the Big Bend there are versions of these stories, which until now have remained in the oral tradition. They are much shorter than those of the Anglo writers. The following account of Carolina, recognizable as another Dolores, was told to me by Samuel Calderón of Fort Davis.

You know the story of Carolina? This Carolina and a young man met at a *baile*—you know, a dance?—and they fell in love. One of the other men said something that reflected on her honor, and Carolina's young man killed him and ran away

to the hills. He agreed with Carolina to burn fires in the hills
to signal each other.

So they burned fires on mountain tops to signal their love
for each other, and he stayed in the mountains herding sheep.
He finally froze to death in a big blizzard.

Then Carolina went crazy and never could understand the
news. For the rest of her life, once a week, she climbed the
mountain to light her fire.

No Indians, no scalping, no coincidence of José's death on
the day before the impending wedding. Such details seem to
be more inherent in the Anglo legend than in the Mexican-
American. Mexican-American traditions, however, are indeed
present. First there is the violence—our hero is a murderer,
and that is why he goes to the hills in hiding. Second, there is
the element of *machismo,* manliness, for it is the hero's duty
to avenge the effrontery shown by the villain toward Carolina.
Melodrama is reduced in a tale like this, wherein the death of
the hero is brought on by forces as mundane as the weather,
instead of by savage Indians, a detail more to be expected in
the "Lover's Leap" kind of tale. An element in common with
the Anglo oral version (but not in Clapp's) is that Carolina
goes insane upon hearing of her lover's death and refuses to
believe that he is dead.

A Mexican-American version of the Indian Emily story
came to me orally and in equally concise form from Mrs.
Celestina Peña of Shafter. She said:

> Dolores was an Indian girl and she was captured and she
> was living with an American family in Fort Davis. When she
> was twenty she fell in love with the boy and, even though she
> was four or five years older than he was, she wanted to marry
> him. He loved her though, you know, as a brother, and he
> married another girl.
>
> Then he was captured and killed by Indians. They burned
> him alive.
>
> So she burned a fire on a hill in his memory every night
> and she lived to be seventy-five years old.
>
> At night you can see her ghost sometimes. It comes down the
> hill and at the foot of the hill it disappears.

Here the two stories have run together, criss-crossed, and mixed details—even the girls' names—to yield what amounts to a third legend based on the two previous ones. Again violence is present in the awful death of the hero, but there is no reference to an attack on the fort. An utterly new detail, of course, is the disparity in ages of the older Dolores (Emily) and the American youth.

The several tellings of the two Fort Davis stories show how they travel along the same road of time in two separate cultures. On this divided highway each set is characterized by narrative techniques that are satisfying to the tale teller and the listener of the particular group. The Mexican-American goes straight to the point in his brief oral account, with little adornment of character and event. Heir to the Victorian heritage, the Anglo writer invents dramatic coincidence, romanticizes the characters, and sentimentalizes their feelings and relationships. In keeping with his heritage of scientific objectivity, he notices little facts that might give even the shakiest credence to his legends. Most important, however, is that, no matter who the tale teller is or how he works, these two Fort Davis legends make good stories.

8.

John Glanton, Scalp Hunter

WITHOUT question the meanest rakehell ever to roam the Big Bend was John Joel Glanton. His trade was killing Indian men, women, and children so as to turn in their scalps for bounty money. He cheated by ripping off and selling the hair of Mexican citizens also. Though not much is heard about Glanton today, in his time he was a grisly living legend.

Apparently the only account of Glanton's early years is what Samuel E. Chamberlain picked up by hearsay when, according to him, he rode with the Glanton gang in Sonora and Arizona. It seems that Glanton was born in South Carolina and as a boy came with his parents to Texas, where he grew up in Stephen F. Austin's colony. Perhaps it was there he met Mabry B. ("Mustang") Gray, said to be Glanton's instructor in the Texas Rangers' arts. As a deeply religious youth Glanton walked a path of rigid morality. It was an older and more smelly Glanton who harangued his fellow Indian killers with drunken sermons laced with obscenities before a rack of drying human scalps.

The story of why Glanton became an Indian killer resembles the familiar Indian Hater legend, a tale that has attached itself to several individuals. Young Glanton's bride-to-be in the Austin colony had been orphaned by Lipan Apaches. On a day that the men were at Austin's house in Gonzales talking politics, another band of Lipans killed and scalped the old women and children and carried away the girls, including

Glanton's betrothed. The men chased and killed the Indians, but not before they had tomahawked the young women and scalped them.

"From this tragic scene," says Chamberlain, "Glanton returned a changed man. He would often absent himself from the village and when he returned he invariably brought fresh scalps." Too close for credibility is this parallel with other stories like it. That of Colonel John Moredock is told by Herman Melville in *The Confidence Man*, and another such tale, of Jeff Turner, is found in John C. Duval's *The Adventures of Big-Foot Wallace*.

After the Indian raid, Glanton became a drunkard and a companion of the roughest desperadoes. During the war of Texas Independence he fought as a "free scout" attached to Colonel James W. Fannin's command. Like John C. Duval, he narrowly escaped the mass execution at Goliad. Rumor said that in battle he always skinned the hair off his Mexican victims and that he owned a mule load of these scalps, smoke dried in his cabin on the Guadalupe. During the Moderator and Regulator fracas, he took neither side but challenged and killed partisans of both factions out of sheer blood lust.

Whatever the exact origin of John Glanton, he must have been born about 1820, and tradition says that at fifteen he was a protege of Texas Ranger Mustang Gray. We are told that Gray instructed him in the roping and taming of wild horses and also in hunting, trailing, fighting, and scalping both Indians and Mexicans. At sixteen Glanton was captain of his own company of Rangers, riding with the infamous "Cow-Boys," who in the 1840s slaughtered South Texas Mexicans wholesale in the whiplash violence that followed the Texas revolt. President Sam Houston declared him an outlaw, but the people held him in such awe and respect that they would not move against him.

Official records tell of Glanton's 1846 marriage, ironically into a respected San Antonio family. He was wed to Joaquina Menchaca, daughter of San Jacinto hero José Menchaca, who also served as a diplomat for President Mirabeau B. Lamar. During the time Joaquina carried and bore their two children, John William, born in 1847, and Joaquina Margarita, 1849, their father was known in San Antonio as a violent killer. Julius Froebel heard that he "shot ten men for sport on the high road." One day he got roaring drunk, tried to kill a preacher, and almost killed two. In an argument over a building lot, Glanton was riled by Presbyterian minister John McCullough. He rode to the minister's house, which was shared by a Methodist preacher, James Young. Glanton rode his horse right into Young's apartment, threw down on him, fired, and missed. Young fled. Seeing his mistake, Glanton rode out to another door, which his intended prey opened. The bullet tore through Rev. John McCullough's hat. The Reverend slammed the door, and another bullet tore splinters through it and again through the hat. Now Glanton saw the Methodist looking on from a distance and took a second wild shot at him. Complaints were filed, and John Glanton was released on bond. As Froebel put it, this man "was one of the most reckless and wicked of a band of murderers and gamblers, who for many years made San Antonio one of the most dangerous places."

It was in San Antonio's Bexar Exchange, a saloon, that Sam Chamberlain first saw him, playing euchre for drinks with another man. Glanton, short, built solid, and burned brown by the sun, peered out of deep-set and bloodshot eyes; his coarse black hair writhed in snakelike hanks down his back and also formed equally ferocious mustachio and beard. He wore a leather jacket blackened by grease and blood and a serape over his shoulders.

A dispute in the game arose, and Glanton splashed a glass of whiskey in his opponent's face. This tall ranger rose and pressed the muzzle of his Navy Colt against Glanton's breastbone, swore an oath or two, and demanded, "If you don't apologize I'll blow a hole through you a jack rabbit could jump through."

The desperado sat quietly, glared at his opponent, and

said, "Shoot and be damned. But if you miss, John Glanton won't miss you."

Now aware of whom he was threatening, the tall ranger was terrified. He pulled the trigger, but only the cap exploded. Instantly Glanton's Bowie knife sliced the ranger's neck half through. The dead man fell in the puddle of his own blood. Glanton scrambled over the table and stood with one foot on his victim.

"Strangers!" he called. "Do you wish to take up this fight? If so, step out. If not, we'll drink."

Everybody headed for the bar and touched glasses with the killer. It was, of course, an act of self-defense. The corpse was carried out, sawdust was scattered to conceal the mess on the floor, and Glanton wiped the blood from his knife on a sleeve of his leather jacket.

This was in 1846. With the onset of the Mexican War, Glanton was enrolled, January, 1847, as a private in Major Walter Lane's company of Texas Cavalry, U.S. Army. The Texas Cavalry were well mounted, not uniformed, armed to the teeth with firearms and Bowie knives and to the eyebrows with terrifying whiskers and hair. General Zachary Taylor often was exasperated by their overenthusiasm both in battle and out. He reported that "the mounted men from Texas have scarcely made one expedition without unaccountably killing a Mexican."

On one occasion Old Rough and Ready was vexed especially with John Glanton. This ranger was riding with a squad detailed to capture or kill a supposed Mexican force amassing at Madelina, near Monterey. As they scouted a street, an armed Mexican galloped toward them. He yelled, *"Carajo a Americanos!"* (Dump on the Americans!), and galloped away. Mounted on a race horse, Glanton chased him down and told him to halt or he would kill him. Either the Mexican could not understand Glanton's words or he ignored the order. Glanton shot him dead and took his horse.

Next day Madelina's mayor complained bitterly to Lane

about Glanton's murdering an innocent man, and Lane gave the mayor the horse, to be returned to the dead man's family. Just outside Monterey, when Lane tried to report of his Madelina action to General Taylor, the general was boiling mad.

"You and your command are a set of robbers and cutthroats!" he cried. "The governor of Madelina has written that you murdered that man in cold blood, that you refused to pay a cent for provisions, and that you all act in a manner unbecoming to United States soldiers."

"It's all a lie."

"Bring me that murderer John Glanton immediately and in irons."

"I'm not going to do it. Glanton was obeying orders. If anybody's to be punished, I'm the one. I gave the order."

"Sir, do you refuse to obey my command?"

"I most emphatically do. Furthermore, you're a general and I'm a little major. But I won't stand here any longer and hear my men and myself abused as robbers and cutthroats."

Touching the brim of his sombrero to the general, Major Lane turned and walked away.

"Halt!" the general commanded.

Still walking, Lane said, "I've heard enough and I decline to hear any more."

"Halt, sir! I place you under arrest."

"I'll see about that!" Lane called back as he mounted Old Buncombe and pounded up dust toward his camp. He went straight to John Glanton.

"John," he said, "you better skip to San Antone. General Taylor's bound to have your scalp, and I can't protect you. Get away now! In half an hour I'll be under arrest myself."

In minutes Glanton had saddled Old Charley and was headed for north of the border. In half an hour a colonel came, too late to arrest him. After a few days General Taylor, in a grumbled apology to Major Lane, suggested that he had acted hastily. In September Glanton was transferred to the

First Regiment of Jack Hays' Texas Mounted Volunteers. Under Hays, Glanton rode with Big Foot Wallace and perhaps with his old friend Mustang Gray, who is said to have led his own volunteer company of "Mustangers." In April, 1848, he was mustered out.

Sometimes the story goes that after the Mexican War, Glanton was lured by the abundance of gold in California. If that was his destination, he took a round about way of getting there. It is said that he hit on the scheme of paying his travel expenses by exterminating Indians along the route and collecting bounty money for their scalps. Whatever his motive, he did form a scalp-hunting gang.

In 1849 a Brazoria County citizen in Chihuahua said that John Glanton and about thirty Texans formed a troop and offered their service to Chihuahua State authorities. The rationale was that ranches in northern Mexico long had suffered depredation by Apaches and by the Comanches before them. Especially during the rainy autumn, Indians from the United States swarmed down the Comanche Trail to cross the Rio Grande at the Big Bend—usually at Lajitas—to rustle livestock and to capture women and children to augment their population. To discourage them, bounties authorized by the legislature were said to be $200 per warrior scalp and $100 per scalp of a woman or a child. A higher reward of $150 was offered for live children under fourteen and for women prisoners, both to be put into peonage. As there is no evidence that Glanton ever brought in a live captive, the extra $50 must not have been worth it to him. Horace Bell says that he was financed to the tune of $2,000 by three Americans in Chihuahua: merchant Horace Riddle, resident John Abel, and the U.S. consul. It must be assumed that these men were to be repaid, with an added cut, from Glanton's recipets.

In addition to the bounty, the troop could keep all the booty they captured, and in a short time they had Indian regalia and weapons enough to disguise themselves as a band of the very enemy they fought. Painted and costumed as Apaches, they assaulted Mexicans with impunity to rob and to scalp.

Though Glanton's operation may have helped Mexican ranchers and farmers somewhat, it aroused disgust in many of his own countrymen. While Governor Angel Trias of Chihuahua complained to American authorities that Ben Leaton near Presidio was selling Indians guns to pillage his state, Leaton was complaining that Glanton was inflaming Indians against all Americans, including himself. In his hunts Glanton was expected to cover some two hundred miles, mostly in the Big Bend between Boquillas and El Paso. As a result, said the Brazoria correspondent, "the Apache, who had been friendly to emigrants, became exceedingly hostile and swore vengeance." U.S. Army General George M. Brooke complained to Washington that Glanton's Chihuahua arrangement led the Indians to believe that it had the approval of the Great White Father in Washington, D.C. So disturbing was Glanton to American-Indian-Mexican relations that Major Jefferson Van Horne requested that Governor Trias either seize Glanton and deliver him to United States officers or permit a detachment of U.S. troops to enter Chihuahua and capture him.

Composed of a few outcast and renegade Texas Rangers along with murderous riffraff from all over the Northern Hemisphere, the Glanton bunch went after Indians armed with revolvers, scalping knives, a disdain for death, a criminal camaraderie, and a will in each to outslaughter his fellows. The route of their foray through the Big Bend became a legend that left its trace on a map copied in 1876 from what may have been an original dated 1857. To judge by this distorted representation of West Texas, the "Rout Taken by John Glanton in Search of Indians" forms a misshapen hourglass with three bulbs. Starting from an abandoned ranch on the Rio Conchos in Mexico, Glanton seems to have passed through San Carlos, Mexico, to cross the Rio Grande at Lajitas. He followed roughly what is now the Big Bend National Park road eastward to the vicinity of Panther Junction. He then cut a path northeastward through the Santiago Mountains and across that still roadless territory to the Pecos, fording it at what is now Iraan. Then he turned back to cross the Pecos at Horsehead Crossing near the McCamey area. From that point he followed the Comanche Trail southwestward to Comanche Spring (Fort Stockton), Burgess Water Hole (Alpine), and down the trail to Panther Junction again. Glanton then swung eastward to "a bold stream," perhaps Tornillo Creek near Boquillas, site of an extremely large and old Indian camp. From that point the trail goes westward south of the Chisos Mountains, back up about to what is now the Camino del Río. This trail took Glanton with his men and their load of scalps to Fort Leaton, represented on the map with a tower and a waving flag. Then it was back into Mexico at Presidio del Norte to hit the road for Chihuahua.

Along this route were plenty of Indian camps. Still to be seen in the Big Bend are campsites marked by fire-blackened rock shelters and circles of stones the Apaches built as supports upon which to erect their brush wickiups. They are to be found especially at the mouths of Tornillo Creek and of Capote Creek where they meet the Rio Grande and between them along Terlingua Creek as well. Calling him "one of the most notoriously cold-blooded ruffians that ever lived," Colonel Richard Irving Dodge says that Glanton discovered "an immense Apache winter camp on the American side of the Grand Canyon of the Rio Grande," as Santa Helena Canyon once was called. "He attacked one end of this camp at daylight one morning, and so scattered were the Indians and so difficult the ground, that his command took (it was said) over two hundred and fifty scalps before the Indians could concentrate in sufficient force to make it prudent for him to retire." After this fight Major Van Horne learned at Fort Leaton that Glanton escaped with great difficulty. In November of 1849 Glanton supposedly was in Juárez after a fight in which Apache chief Gómez was killed.

Back in Chihuahua with his first harvest, Glanton is said to have been received and honored at the governor's palace and to have led a parade of his cutthroats through arches of triumph. The record does not say if the reception hall still was festooned with Indians' ears as it was reputed to be in 1843 when the scalp hunter honored was James Kirker, called by the Mexicans Santiago Querque. With some formality Glanton delivered the blood-flecked skins to a government agent, was paid, then was feasted and lionized by leading citizens. After a month of fiesta, John Glanton was ready to ride out with his men on a second foray.

By one or both of these raids Glanton aroused the wrath of his former commander, Jack Hays. Traveling toward Arizona to assume the post of Indian sub-agent on the Gila River, Hays persuaded Glanton to swear he would not disturb Indains along the route to Tucson before Hays had a chance to treat with them. Hays got no farther than Franklin (now El Paso). The following January (1850) Hays reported in his letter of resignation, "As a large portion of this tribe [Apaches] were living on the Rio Grande below and above Presidio del Norte, I sought to have an interview. They were shy and hostile, with feeling aroused against the whites by an attack recently made on them by some Americans employed by the Governor of Chihuahua, expressly to fight Indians." Glanton's word was hollow.

The second roving engagement in Indian killing seems to have been even more productive than the first. For a time Glanton and his men were heroes of the north of Mexico, but ugly rumors spread. They said Glanton was running out of Indians and was killing defenseless Mexican citizens, tearing off their scalps and trimming them to look like the real thing. Also, the Texans in the party were suspected of hating Mexicans more than they hated Indians. The authorities could not tolerate a growing belief that they were unable to distinguish the hair of a fellow citizen from that of an Apache. They called Glanton in, hotly reprimanded him, and fired him. He and his men swore innocence, but they were aware that the Juez de Cordada—vigilante justice—was hardening against them. There is no trial at the Juez de Cordada; the people simply mob the suspect and pound him to death with bottles and rocks. In the night the Indian hunters sneaked out and headed west across the Sierra Madre.

Despite Chihuahuan misgivings about his integrity, Glanton is said to have made a similar but less remunerative arrangement with the state of Sonora. Supposedly he contracted for fifty dollars per scalp with Governor General D. José Urrea, the very man who had tried to kill him along with other Texans at Goliad. Apaches in northern Sonora and in Arizona now were the scalp hunter's quarry.

On one of Glanton's marches as he approached Tucson, says Horace Bell, the little town was under an Apache siege led by Mangas Colorado. As the able-bodied men had gone to hunt gold in California, only a few old men were there to stand off the marauders. Glanton's rangers galloped through the attackers and joined the defenders. Having arranged a parley, Mangas Colorado told Glanton he was surprised that Americans were helping Mexicans. Glanton replied, "Americans always defend the weak, and unless you leave before sunup, we Americans will turn loose our saddles [meaning their holster pistols] on you."

Then Mangas Colorado had an idea. Everybody agreed to his proposal that the Mexicans give up seven head of cattle and plenty of mescal and that they all have a fiesta in the plaza. Then he and his warriors would go in peace. The old chief protested, "I restrain my men from killing Mexicans. For if we kill off the Mexicans, who will raise our cattle and horses for us?"

Either before or after this Tucson adventure the scalp hunters rode into the northeastern Sonora mining town of Jesús María and pitched camp to rest up. For a while they caroused in the cantinas, safe in the tolerance of the local people. As in San Antonio, Glanton got too drunk for his own good. Full of tequila and reeling in his saddle, he galloped into the plaza yelling Texian slogans, hauled down the Mexican flag, tied it to the tail of a mule, whipped the mule into a frenzy, and turned it loose on the town.

Instantly the villagers mobilized and mobbed Glanton, his gang, and two peaceable Americans who lived there. The merchants escaped on foot, and the Glanton bunch rode into the desert and mountains.

When on the march of General L. P. Graham's column across Arizona to California, an artistic young soldier, Sam Chamberlain, was tied up near Tucson as punishment for wasting his time drawing pictures. A disreputable-looking Glanton man sauntered up and nonchalantly cut him down, immediately to be arrested and tied up himself. This was Crying Tom Hitchcock, who would curse and converse in a mixture of English and Spanish (both bad), roar out his "wild and woolly" boasts, bellow like a buffalo bull, and frequently burst into uncontrollable weeping. When Chamberlain said he wished to desert and join the scalp hunters, Crying Tom advised, "Join Satan and go to Hell." At the young man's insistence, however, the desperado consented to take him along. Actually, Crying Tom was one of several recruiters Glanton had sent out from his camp at Frontreras in Sonora to follow the army's column and seduce men into the gang.

Before they reached Frontreras they shot an Indian, who jumped over a cliff to die in a way more of his own choosing. Crying Tom exclaimed, "*Cinquento pesos* gone to hell, *muchacho*. The Goddamn red nigger done that to cheat us out of his hair."

Camped in a cottonwood grove near Frontreras were about forty Indian hunters. Among them were three former soldiers Chamberlain knew with McCulloch's rangers: Ben Tobin, Doc Irving, and Sam Tate. Glanton himself came forward and said, "What in hell have ye got there, Tom? Where were ye spawned, stranger, and where do ye tie up?"

Glanton extended his hand; Chamberlain reached to shake

it, Glanton laughed and grasped the young man's nose, giving it a painful twist. Chamberlain knocked Glanton down with a punch to the face, jumped on his horse, and drew his pistol. In an instant he was lassoed, dragged to the ground, and tied to a tree.

His nose bleeding, Glanton pushed the muzzle of a cocked pistol against Chamberlain's forehead. The two men stared at each other. After a long minute Glanton lowered the pistol, shook Sam's hand, and said, "Real grit, stranger. Ye'll pass. Ye strike like the kick of a burro."

Now with some leisure to look about him Chamberlain saw thirty-seven scalps drying out, each "cut with the right ear on to prevent fraud, as some Indians have two circles to their hair." There was $1,850 right there.

Next day when Glanton rode off with a group to La Villa de Mapimi to collect bounty money from a government agent, Chamberlain observed scalp-hunter camp life. The men drank, danced, and whored. Gigantic Judge Holden of Texas—friend and confidante of Glanton—raped and murdered a ten-year-old girl. (An expert horseman and a crack shot, this Holden was a well-educated man who played the guitar and harp and was versed in geology, mineralogy, botany, and several Indian languages.)

When Glanton returned five days later, he had no money and three of his men were wounded. Disguised as Apaches, they had attacked a camp of Mexicans. They killed and scalped three men, knocked three women in the head because they were old and ugly and also scalped them. Their only booty was two young women and a few blankets. Next day they camped, got drunk, and raped the girls. When avenging Mexicans attacked that night, they brained the girls and rode to safety through the ranks of their assailants. Glanton had reaped eight more scalps, bringing up his take to forty-five—$2,250.

After a parley, the gang agreed that they could make more money in the California gold-mining country. Crying

Tom volunteered to ride to Mapimi to cash in the scalps, and off he set with Marcus L. ("Long") Webster and a half Cherokee, Charley McIntosh. A few days later this team rejoined the gang at Ojo de Conejo in Arizona, happy because they successfully had cashed in the Mexican scalps as well as the Apache. They brought ammunition, pinole, and El Paso whiskey. At the ensuing Saturnalia the gang gorged on barbecued beef, stolen locally.

During this party, the wildly drunk Glanton started to preach. Larding his sermon with brimstone curses, he cried out that all his gang were damned sinners headed for eternal Hell. He shouted that his mission was to save them, then knelt and solemnly uttered a long, fervent prayer for the souls of his cutthroats. Suddenly he leaped up, drew his pistol, and blasted away repeatedly at his men. One of the Canadians fell with a bullet in his leg. Big Judge Holden seized Glanton, forced him to the ground, and with his arms around him, soothed him as a mother would quiet a child.

By this time Sam Chamberlain was convinced that John Glanton was insane. (Duval's Jeff Turner confessed, "I am more like a crazy man than anything else, when I have to go a long time without lifting a scalp.") On the trail again, the changeable Glanton's scheme now was to find the legendary Seven Cities of Cíbola, said to be built of pure gold and inhabited by white Indians. His superstitious rangers fell in with the hope of plundering that metropolis. After days on the blistering desert march in Arizona, Glanton stopped at the top of a ridge and exclaimed, "El Dorado at last, by God!"

The men rushed forward to see what appeared to be a maze of golden towers and walls rising from the desert floor. Judge Holden laughed, "So Glanton, this is El Dorado, is it? The city of gold and fair women! I wish you joy of the discovery—a city of sandstone built by nature." Mounting a rock for a platform, the judge delivered a lecture on geology, including the statement, "Millions of years have witnessed the operation producing the result around us."

Still in tune with part of his fundamentalist Bible learning, Glanton interjected, "That's a damn lie!"

Now the journey to their original destination, California,
was resumed. They encountered a large band of Indians, and
when the skirmishes were over, fourteen of Glanton's men
were missing, and of the twenty-four remaining, seven were
badly wounded. Glanton ordered Judge Holden and Doc
Irving to determine which of the wounded were unable to
ride. When they reported the names of four, Glanton declared
it would be a mercy to them and a better guarantee of safety
to the others if these men died. "It's the law of the desert," he
said. For the drawing of lots to see who would execute which
of the wounded, twenty Apache arrows were placed in a coyote skin quiver, four of them marked. Sam Tate drew the one
marked for Dick Shelby, a young Kentuckian. Long Webster
was to execute the Sonoran. A Delaware Indian volunteered
to kill his two fellow Delawares.

Next morning the gang rode out of camp, leaving the
executioners each with an Apache war club at the side of his
wounded victim. Glanton signaled by firing his pistol. The
men could hear the crunch of administered death. The living
headed for the gold fields, sick and guilty in spirit.

Blocked by Grand Canyon, they changed their route and
came at last to the Gila River, running flush. Seeing a village
of Pimas on the other side, Glanton's Indian hatred flared up.
He wanted to cross over and annihilate the entire village, but
his gang voted him down. After two days in the settlement,
where the Indians supplied the rangers with flour, beans, and
pumpkins, Glanton got roaring drunk by pouring stale agave
juice down his throat. Some of the men—by now it was routine—lassoed him and tied him down for the night. Then
Judge Holden went wild again, grabbed a Pima girl, and was
about to rape her when a dozen cocked scalp-hunter rifles
aimed at his person caused him to desist.

Next day the hung-over John Glanton led the scalp hunters out of the Pima village, heading for the Gila's junction

with the mighty Colorado. There they rested for two days, recruiting themselves and their mounts for the *jornada del muerto* across 130 miles of the scorching, waterless sand of Southern California.

About two miles below the mouth of the Gila, Sam Chamberlain scouted Yuma Indians operating two ferry boats made of U.S. Army wagon beds. When Sam told Glanton about the ferry, an old chief showed Glanton a paper signed by General Graham, making him a gift of the boats for services rendered. Then Glanton and Judge Holden put their heads together in a long, confidential conference.

Next morning Glanton addressed the men. "This ferry is our El Dorado, our gold mine," he said and went on to propose that they take it, kill the Indians if they resisted, and capture all the young women. The majority voted approval, plans were studied, and on the same day at a signal from Glanton they seized both boats and nine of the prettiest Yuma girls. After tying the girls hand and foot, they constructed a circular stone barricade on a nearby hill, which Glanton called Fort Defiance, in memory of the barricade he had helped Fannin build at Goliad.

All night Indians hung around the scalp-hunter barricade. Next day at noon, four warriors advanced ahead of the band, calling, "Amigo! Amigo!" With three of his men, Glanton went out to meet them, armed with concealed revolvers. The Yumas wanted their boats, the girls, and the departure of the desperadoes. Glanton replied, "We're going to keep all we took, and if you don't supply me with beans and bunch grass, I'm going to destroy your village and kill everybody in it."

The four Indians whipped out clubs, rushed Glanton's delegation swinging, and were all felled by Glanton pistols. From force of habit, Glanton and his men ripped the skin from their heads. Howling with rage and despair, the mass of Yumas retreated and for several days gave no trouble. They were watching and planning. During this respite, Glanton's

Mitre Peak north of Alpine, said to have been named "La Mitra" by the devil when he was cast out of heaven. (Photo by Charles Hunter.)

Inside the devil's cave overlooking Ojinaga, Mexico, and Presidio, Texas, with the Chinati Mountains to the north. (Photo by Glenn Burgess.)

Nieves Samaniego inside the shrine on El Cerrito de la Santa Cruz. The cross is supposedly the one Father Urbán used to drive the devil from the valley. (Photo by Glenn Burgess.)

The devil's ball on Saragosa Street in Ojinaga, Mexico. (Photo by Glenn Burgess.)

Left: Nuestro Padre Jesús, the image in the church at Ojinaga Mexico.

Right: Eighteenth-century painting in the Ojinaga church with a narrative about the jointed Cristo. (Photo by Helen Adams, Folklore Collection, English Department, Sul Ross State University.)

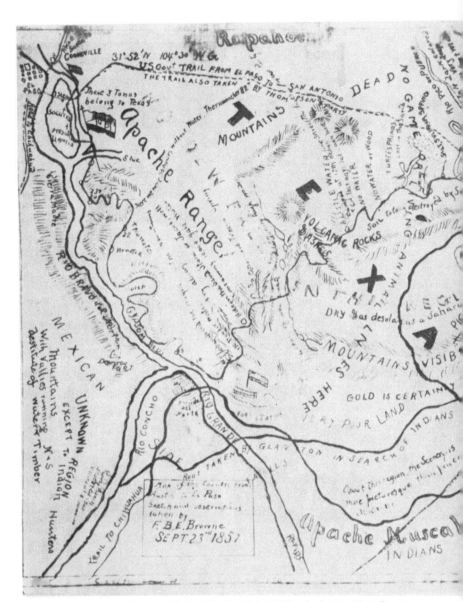

A forty-niner's map of the Big Bend in 1851, depicting Fort Leaton and the "Rout Taken by Glanton in Search of Indians." (Courtesy, Shipman Collection, Archives of the Big Bend, Sul Ross State University.)

The face of Alsate, one of the Chisos ghosts. (Photo by Peter Koch.)

Fort Leaton, the north side. (Courtesy, W. D. Smithers Collection, Humanities Research Center, University of Texas at Austin.)

Bobcat Carter in cold weather, wearing several layers of old socks.
(Courtesy, William A. Cooper.)

Bobcat Carter at home inside his tin shed back of Cooper's Store.
(Courtesy, William A. Cooper.)

A time exposure of Marfa Lights against the Chinatis on the horizon across Mitchell Flat. There are at least five lights, one moving. (Courtesy, Carl Appel.)

men ferried over several parties of Mexicans heading for the gold fields at the inflated charge of four dollars per person and one dollar for each of the animals, which were tied alongside the boats.

The story of the ferry as told by John Russell Bartlett adds some details and leaves out others when his hearsay version is compared with that of Sam Chamberlain, who claimed to be a participant. Bartlett says that Glanton brought thirteen bandits to the Colorado River, where he ran the ferry for a Dr. Langdon, who was managing it for J. P. Brolis of Sonora. When Glanton took charge, he hiked the rate to four dollars per person and imposed even greater charges on Mexicans returning home from California if he thought they had gold. When Dr. Langdon tried to fire Glanton, Glanton would not quit. Omitted from Bartlett's version is any word of Glanton's having captured the boats from the Yumas, nor does Bartlett say why the Yumas later attacked Fort Defiance. Chamberlain's version gives them ample reason.

Shortly after going into the ferry business (says Chamberlain), Glanton rode to California with three companions, taking along a thousand dollars to buy beef. Ten days later Glanton returned and—as before in Mexico—with no money and no beef. He was driving, however, a mule load of whiskey and had fetched a few pounds of coffee, sugar, and hardtack. His companions had deserted him. In San Diego, he said, he got in trouble and killed two soldiers. Now, he said, he had a profitable friendship with a party of Sonorans, heading home across the desert with plenty of gold. He proposed that the gang waylay and rob them, and of course kill them while they were about it.

All hands refused. When his own men told him he was going too far, Glanton tired to pass off the proposition as a joke. That night he and his fifteen men (Chamberlain's figure) lightened the mule's burden of whiskey as much as they could. Drinking less and plotting desertion were Crying Tom Hitchcock, Ben Tobin, and Long Webster, with Sam Chamberlain their ring leader. Early next morning Chamberlain and his three companions came together at their rendezvous.

At the same moment, Yumas armed with stone hatchets were sneaking into the makeshift Fort Defiance. Shrewdly they had waited for the inevitable orgy that would leave the men snoring in the grip of a colossal hangover. At a signal the Indians started yelling and clubbing. "The bluff on which the fort was built," said Chamberlain, "was covered with howling Indians."

Crying Tom exclaimed, "Glanton's rubbed out, by God!"

A renegade priest, Tobin raised his sombrero and said to Sam, "It's the hand of God! To Him and you, His blind instrument, we owe our lives."

For whatever poetic justice it is worth, Bartlett says that, after smashing the skulls of the scalp hunters, the Indians scavenged somewhere between fifteen and thirty thousand dollars from their pockets.

Soon the deserters were joined by the despised Judge Holden, and, now five in number, they nudged their horses into that horrible blow-sand desert, heading for San Diego. Before they reached that town, they left Holden behind in a friendly Indian village. Chamberlain ends his story here, but it may be that he was one of three who turned up in San Diego deposing to be deserters from the U.S. Army and members of the Glanton gang. If so, Marcus L. Webster (Long Webster) seems to have given his right name, while the other two signed themselves as William Carr and Joseph Anderson. Chamberlain may have been one of these two. To finish Sam Chamberlain's life story, he is thought to have served with filibuster William Walker in Nicaragua. Afterward he became a policeman in Boston, served as a Civil War soldier, was promoted to general, and finally enjoyed a long career as a warden in Connecticut state prisons. Surely he knew the kind of men under his charge.

The way Horace Bell heard it, only two—not five—escaped the Fort Defiance massacre. He says that Dave and Charley Brown (neither mentioned by Chamberlain) left camp at dawn after the big drunk, each with an iron kettle to fetch water. While they were dipping from the Colorado, Yumas under Chief Pasqual surrounded the stone fence, attacked, and killed everybody. When the Brown boys saw what was happening, they jumped aboard one of the boats and let her float down stream. A few miles down they landed and started trudging through the blistering sand toward the coast, each lugging an iron kettle of water. The water soon played out, and they were walking skeletons when they staggered into San Diego. Charley Brown died in Nicaragua in Walker's invasion, and in Los Angeles Dave Brown went up the rope laughing, as he was being hanged by a bunch of drunken rowdies just for fun anyway.

The clash of three cultures helped to make John Glanton and his followers what they were. Along the Rio Grande occurred the encounter of the Anglo-American, the Spanish-Mexican, and the Plains Indian cultures. This clash provided a function in the early frontier society for the criminal and the homicidal maniac, who in the eastern settlements either would have been hanged or locked up in an asylum. Before 1850 killers like John Glanton served the Anglo-American and the Spanish-Mexican societies decisively, if not well, by their actions against the Indians. Thus a bloody-minded, compulsive murderer like John Glanton could exist by official and even by some popular sanction until the tide turned against him and his kind. By 1850 the scalp hunters were so successful, the Indians were so thoroughly intimidated, and the reservation system had become so effective that scalp hunters and the old kind of Indian-hunting ranger were no longer needed. The Indian Hater was a hero no more.

Many a reader and listener among us folk, however, still appeases a deep-down blood lust with rip-roaring tales about some obscenely mutilating killer, upon whom some vile restlessness of our own unspeakable subconscious can project itself. For that comforting function, no more satisfactory subject exists than John Glanton.

9.
Bobcat Carter

NOBODY knew where he came from exactly or how he stayed alive. They said he looked as old in 1908 as he did in 1940. Called Bobcat Carter, he was one of the most unusual characters in the Big Bend, where the unique is more to be expected than not.

About six feet tall and with lively blue eyes, the wiry old man lived in a tin shed at the back of Cooper's Store, which used to do business near Persimmon Gap. With the shaggy and statuesque face of an honored general of earlier days, Carter wore indiscriminate rags, a ruined hat, and sometimes castoff brogans. He told Hallie Stillwell, "Cleanliness is next to Godliness. A man ought to take a bath every seven years whether he needs it or not. I do." Frank Wedin of Marathon called him "that nasty old devil that lived at Persimmon Gap," and Guy Lee, of the same place, said, "I would just as soon of smelled a polecat as old Carter."

All who saw him attested to his abundant health. He walked everywhere he went. He was never known to ride a horse or a burro, though he would accept and sometimes flag a ride in a car or wagon. In the 1930s, when he lived at Cooper's Store, he would waylay travelers by energetic waving, singing, and prancing at the side of the road, sometimes turning handsprings. Though he was called a hermit, he loved company, and he became one of the standard Big Bend tourist attractions. On a slow day, when travelers were infrequent, he would cavort in the middle of the road, making it impossible for a car to pass until its passengers stopped for a visit.

Many vacationers looked forward to the encounter and would offer Carter eggs or a can of beans from their store of camp groceries, and he is not known ever to have refused. Tourists would take snapshots of Carter and of themselves standing with him, and after returning home they often would send him a copy. These Bobcat Carter photographs are now in the possession of William (Bill) A. Cooper, Jr., of Snyder. It was his father, W. A. Cooper, who ran the store and provided the garrulous old loner his last dwelling place.

Most of what is known about the old man was gathered by Ross Burns of Anson, Texas. Henry F. Carter claimed that he was born in Springfield, Missouri, on September 9, 1843. As it is contrary to custom in the Big Bend to inquire about anybody's past, little is known of his history. Bill Cooper remembered that Carter said something about the "rough boys" back home, adding that he never rode with them. Cooper got the impression that some of these rough boys had driven him out of the country. Because Carter never worked for wages or asked for money, Guy Lee thought that he must be hiding out in the Big Bend and that he must have some money to live on hidden away somewhere.

Before 1908 he had drifted to the ranch country around San Angelo and Christoval, where he contracted to poison prairie-dog towns. W. A. Cooper knew him there and said he looked about the same then as he did when he showed up in the Big Bend about 1930. In 1908 he would have been sixty-three years old. While in Tom Green County he acquired the name of Prairie Dog Carter and was said to have eaten the prairie dogs he killed. Whether or not he ate the poisoned meat, he might well have dined on healthy prairie dogs for they are considered a squirrellike delicacy by most who have tried them. Be that as it may, it seems that Carter simply did not much care what he ate.

It is said that after helping to eradicate prairie dogs, Car-

ter went into the Big Bend and into Mexico searching for a
lost gold mine reputed to be somewhere along the Rio Grande
not far from Stillwell Crossing. In 1929 he was joined by a
brother, Dick Carter, and went trapping in Mexico. He crossed
the border opposite Del Rio at Acuña, where he was issued a
Mexican passport. The next anybody knows of the old loner,
his brother was no longer with him, and he was living at various locations in the Big Bend, engaged in trapping bobcats
and other varmints for their skins. Elmo Johnson's trading
post, near the head of Mariscal Canyon, was one of the best-
known places where trappers could sell or trade their skins of
fox, coyote, wildcat, sunk, and sometimes goat. W. D. Smithers has estimated that the average earnings of a trapper like
Carter was about fifty cents a day if he worked hard.

In the Big Bend, because he trapped wildcats and ate
them, the old man came to be known as Bobcat Carter. On
one occasion the Alpine newspaper reported that he trapped
"forty-three bobcats and eleven outlaw house cats in a canyon
near where he lived." Before he grew too old to trap in the
rough country, he dwelled at numerous places, usually in what
Bill Cooper described as a dugout supplemented with "tin,
ducking, tow sacks, just about anything he could find to make
a windbreak." For a time he lived along the Rio Grande. In
the winter of 1931-1932 he stayed on the Henderson ranch,
once he stayed at Guy Lee's ranch for about a week, and Bear
Hollis remembered Carter's living for a while in John Walker's
deserted "fine old house" halfway between Charley Green's
ranch and Persimmon Gap. Nell Davis recalled his residing
somewhere in the mountain-desert country in a makeshift
shack that was partly a tent, with his cot under a brush arbor
in front.

Finally W. A. Cooper felt sorry for the old wanderer and
offered him a place to live at his store, about halfway between
the present Persimmon Gap Ranger Station and Persimmon
Gap itself. As Frank Wedin heard it, he lived first in the base-
ment of the store but wanted out because it leaked during the

infrequent rain storms. There was an old tin shed near the store, Cooper said he could stay in it, and here Bobcat Carter settled down and made a tourist attraction of himself.

Mark Twain would have called Carter "unspeakably picturesque." He dressed in a miscellany of castoff garments he had found or that people had given him, and his shapeless pants usually were held up by suspenders, which in turn were anchored in place with cotton cord. Though he is said to have gone barefoot most of the time, photographs show him with loosely laced and dilapidated work shoes. Sometimes he made huaraches for his feet out of old automobile tires, and for a time he wore a threadbare canvas coat that hung down almost to his knees. Some pictures show him wearing the Texas Centennial hat given to him by W. A. Cooper, which he wore until it fell apart. Others show the straw sombrero to which he gave longer life by loosely sewing pieces of ducking around it.

Carter talked about clothes with Bill Cooper one chilly morning when he hitched a wagon ride with Bill, who was going to fetch a couple of barrels of water for the store. On the subject of how to keep warm, Carter said he never threw away a shirt when the buttons popped off, as many wasteful people do. Instead he just put another shirt on over the old one. That helped keep the cold out. When the toe of a sock wore out, he said, he just shoved his foot through the sock and pulled it up on his leg. To show what he meant, he hoisted a pants leg and revealed to young Cooper about ten or twelve old socks on his shanks. The way he kept his feet warm, he said, was to put pepper in his shoes.

Yet Bobcat Carter had a special set of clothing for the few dress-up occasions in his life. Guy Lee said that though he ordinarily went barefoot and dressed shabbily, it was different on election days. Still not having taken a bath, he would put on his best clothes and his disreputable brogans and walk the forty-five miles to Marathon and back unless he caught a ride.

On his festive days in Marathon, Carter would electioneer

for one candidate or another, always one that was sure to lose. He would prance up and down the main street and, as Hallie Stillwell has said, turn handsprings and annoy voters either approaching the polling place or in it. When Hallie was an election judge, Carter would argue with her and the other judges, demanding his right to vote. W. A. Cooper had managed to get him a county pension of twelve dollars a month, and he was therefore on the pension list. Hallie told Carter that since he was on the pension list, that meant he had signed a pauper's oath and was ineligible to vote. The old man was outraged. He swore up and down that he never signed a pauper's oath in his life and that they had better hand over a ballot. More often than not the election judges finally shoved a ballot at him to make him quit pestering them. Then, after marking his ballot, the "gregarious hermit" would go back on the street and resume making a nuisance of himself with his palaver, handsprings, and somersaults.

Except on election days Carter was usually at his flimsy tin shed. Its only article of furniture seems to have been a homemade rocking chair. Constructed of sticks and twine, it sat outside against the wall on sunny days, which would be almost every day. Carter rested and slept on a cot in a mass of foul bedding. On the dirt floor inside were a barrel and a cable spool serving as tables and some kind of cook stove. Hanging on boards that held the walls together were utensils in the form of old tin cans and cloth bags containing nobody knows what. Guy Lee said he could smell Carter's camp a mile away.

The old man kept chickens and pigs, which provided him with eggs and meat. Sometimes he sold eggs and pigs, which brought a little extra money to buy staples from Cooper's Store. He shot small game with his old hexagon-barrel rifle and still trapped a little. It was said he would eat anything he snared, no matter what. Guy Lee once saw him early in the morning milk one of Lee's mares and drink the milk. Lee strongly suspected that Carter also made off with the colt and ate it.

Only one tale has to do with alcoholic drink. Ross Maxwell heard that the supplier for the Citizens Conservation Corps then working at the Big Bend National Park had a bottle with him when he stopped for a visit. When he offered the old man a drink from an unopened fifth of whiskey, Carter said he was too young to drink and then proceeded to open the bottle and pour its contents down his gullet.

It is said that Carter's home cooking most frequently featured prairie dog stew and bobcat stew. Tom Henderson says that another of his dishes was polecat stew, with potatoes and onions. Once Bear Hollis and Jack Dawson arrived at the camp just before mealtime, and Carter invited them to share his bobcat stew. Jack was so hungry he partook of enough to stay his appetite, but Bear preferred to remain hungry. On another occasion Carter may have been playing a crude joke when he called out to Bill Cooper, who was passing on horseback, and invited him to eat. Still sitting on his horse, Cooper saw Carter lift the lid on the dutch oven to reveal maggots working on its contents. Cooper rode away.

When Virginia Young was a student at Marathon High School, she and some of her friends stopped by Carter's place on their way to the Big Bend Park. They were visiting outside the shed when it began to rain. The old man asked them in for coffee, and they accepted as they often had drunk the coffee from his lidless pot before. This time, however, Virginia noticed several hens roosting on a rafter directly over the uncovered coffee. On this visit she observed common courtesy, but she never drank Bobcat Carter's coffee again.

Sometimes Carter entertained his visitors with singing. The fact that he remembered few words to any of his songs in no way discouraged him, nor did the fact that, according to Bear Hollis, most of his notes were sour. He liked to caterwaul fragments of "The Streets of Laredo," one of his favorites. Ross Burns learned that Bobcat Carter's niece, Mrs. Mertie Spencer, recalled a couple of tunes he taught her when she was a little girl. They were "Paddle Your Own Canoe" and, as Carter pronounced it, "Pattridge is a Pretty Bird."

Bobcat Carter was also remembered for a few gems of the wit and wisdom. Once a woman interviewer asked him how long he had lived in this part of the country, and he replied, "Why, honey, I put the bark on the bushes in the Big Bend." One of his favorite sayings, Bill Cooper remembered, was:

> Sew 'em up, fix 'em up, make 'em do,
> You're better off with the old than in debt for the new.

Another went, "The guy that's furtherest from the market is the guy that ain't got anything to sell." Both of these proverbs applied to himself. When his niece discussed her impending marriage with him, he advised, "Look before you leap, for there might be a snake in the grass."

Christian Science was the source of the only religious tenets Bobcat Carter was known to have embraced. Guy Lee said that once Bobcat made up his mind to believe in something, he was unshakable in the conviction. In 1937 he was sick and asked Mrs. Belle Henderson to help him. She did what she could for him, she gave him some Christian Science pamphlets, and he recovered. He schooled himself somewhat in Christian Science and thereafter had his method of fighting disease. When he was sick with a cold or some minor illness, the Coopers, having gone to his assistance, would find him lying on his cot repeating, "Mind over matter—mind over matter" to himself.

When the news went round that Bobcat Carter was dead, there were those who did not wish to believe it. They preferred to say that when he left the Big Bend, he just left. Perhaps it was his liveliness and his relish for life that makes us admire and even envy him despite his eccentric ways.

In 1940 he got very sick, the Coopers took him to the hospital in Alpine, and there he died on October 14 of "hypostatic pneumonia, aided by senility" at the age of ninety-seven. Some believe his death was caused by an enforced violation of his lifestyle. When he arrived at the hospital, they say, the first thing they did was give Bobcat Carter a bath and that is what killed him.

10.

The Lost
Haystack Mine

SHAPED roughly like the object it is named for, Haystack Mountain stands to the west of Mitre Peak (where the devil made his landing when ejected from Heaven) a few miles northwest of Alpine. In the Haystack Mountain neighborhood of bunch grass and purple-flowering cholla cactus, there is said to be a lost gold mine. Unless of course, as some others say, it lies about fifty miles to the south at Santiago Peak in the bunch grass and white-blossomed sotol country. Or maybe the mine is much closer to Alpine, in Sunny Glen. The likelihood is that this lucrative digging exists only in the tales told about it in the Big Bend country. It is probable, however, that in the 1930s something involving a chunk of bull quartz did happen which stirred keen interest in the lost mine, imaginary or not.

Whatever happened is said to have involved a Negro, who arrived in Alpine once a year to walk an untrackable path into the mountains and come back with gold. Then he would return to his home in San Antonio, where he cashed in his raw wealth. Of the several versions of this tale, each seeming to have a life of its own, most share details with yarns about the Lost Nigger Mine and the Lost Dutchman Mine as well as with each other. Like its counterparts the Lost Haystack Mine has been untiringly sought by several of Coronado's Children, as J. Frank Dobie called those obsessed with the search for riches hidden in the earth or to be mined.

One of the older tales has it simply that years ago an

Indian living deep in the southern Big Bend country did his trading in Alpine and always paid in gold dust. His affluence aroused covetousness in some of the local men, who set out several times to follow him secretly, only to be invariably thrown off the track. After several years the Indian ceased to appear in Alpine, but effort still was made to line out his trail and to locate the gold mine, always without success.

Alike in some details is the story heard by Barton Warnock of Alpine in 1937 when he was an undergraduate at what is now Sul Ross State University. In the account Barton heard, a Negro would appear in Alpine about once a year, then disappear south of town and return with gold nuggets. A few greedy souls tracked him to Santiago Peak and saw him go into his mine. Overjoyed, they came back to town and waited until the Negro had left the country. When they returned to help themselves to all that gold, they could not pick up their own trail and never found the mine again. This same Barton Warnock already had heard a similar story in Odessa in about 1931. Once a year a man came to Odessa, would go into the sandhills toward the Guadalupe Mountains, and return with gold nuggets. He too was trailed and also shook off his followers.

In about 1937 the talk around Alpine barber shops and pool rooms carried gossip of what may be called the Lost Haystack Mine. As tales are apt to do, this one attached itself to several local ranchers and workmen in the Big Bend.

What specifically stirred up this legend and fastened it onto various people may have been a real piece of bull quartz. It was seen and handled by prospector Art Gard, who owned mineral claims all over Texas and traded in used furniture in order to support his family. He told me that the elusive Negro gave the owner of the Sunny Glen land (about five miles northwest of Alpine) this chunk of rock. He in turn gave it to the next owner of the land, Clarence Hord, who showed it to Art and asked Art's opinion about it. Art said it was bull quartz with signs of gold—it was glassy and white, not milky or pink like most quartz. Bull quartz, Art said, is found in great quantity wherever it is located, and any metal associated with it—gold in this case—also is usually present in great quantity.

Responding to his prospector's instinct, Art spent an entire month systematically combing Sunny Glen and found no such bull quartz deposit. Meanwhile Clarence Hord had a chemical analysis made of his fragment, and the general conclusion was that no deposit of such quartz has been found anywhere in the Big Bend country.

As Art heard it from Clarence Hord and others, a Negro herding sheep in Sunny Glen found a cache of this gold-yielding quartz. The amount of ore hidden may have been a single burro load or a whole burro train load, depending on who was telling the story. After moving to San Antonio, this Negro would return once a year and get off the train at Tornato, the first stopping place west of Alpine. He would hike north toward the mountains and return to the Tornato sign with a batch of ore on the same day in time to catch the next train back to San Antonio. He would fetch out only enough ore to yield him a modest living until he returned twelve months later. Acquisitive men tracked him and put hounds on his trail with no luck. As far as Art knew, the Negro gave the piece of quartz to the Sunny Glen owner and tried unsuccessfully to make some sort of business deal with him. One day the black man left Tornato with a smaller amount of the stuff than he had carried out the year before, and he never returned.

That is the way Art Gard heard it. Now here are two ways I heard it in chairs at opposite ends of the same barber shop, one from Bill Lane and the other from his brother Buddy Lane, both of whom were barbering at that time.

Bill said that along about 1930 Clarence Hord and his brother Alonzo were mighty interested in what they said was a gold strike that a Negro claimed he had found on their Sunny Glen ranch. When Alonzo told Bill about it, he was so angry he was almost grinding his teeth. He said the Negro lived in San Antonio, that he had not seen him in quite some time, and also that the Negro better not let him catch up with him either. It seemed to Bill that Alonzo was ready to do harm to the Negro, either to get a full share of the gold or because the Negro had cheated him somehow.

Two chairs down and about two weeks later, Buddy laughed about the story and said, "They all tell it on each other." As he heard it, there was once a northern Yankee Negro stationed at Fort D. A. Russell, twenty-five miles west of Alpine at Marfa. He was friendly with a black woman who cooked on the Gage ranch, and he would walk out there to call on her. From these amorous visits he would return with a batch of gold ore and somehow sell it in San Antonio. After his discharge from the army, this black man made annual gold trips to the Sunny Glen–Haystack area. He was of course tracked, and as usual he eluded his trackers, though once they did run across a small digging, where a shovel and a bucket had been left behind.

As this particular Negro had settled in Austin, not San Antonio, the white seekers betook themselves to Austin to confront the discoverer. They threatened to kill him if he did not divulge the whereabouts of his gold, but he defiantly refused to tell them anything. They discovered his buyer in San Antonio and did their best to pry the details from him, but he would not talk either.

Yet another story came from Joe Brady, another former prospector of Alpine, who found more profit in selling automobile tires. Into his story has entered that imagination-snaring object the treasure map. According to Joe, a Negro worked as a chauffeur for somebody in Marfa. When this chauffeur died he left to his brother, "who lived up north," a map charting the location of a gold deposit. It took the heir three years to find the place, but when he did he suddenly was a rich man, and following his discovery his annual visits began. He would ride the train to Alpine, rent a cab before daylight, drive west on Highway 90, stop about sunrise, and have the driver to wait on the shoulder. Then the Negro hiked north toward Haystack

Mountain with an empty black bag in his hand. About noon he returned to the cab, puffing from the heavy weight in the bag. Then the cab took him back to Alpine, where he caught the eastbound train. Somebody in Alpine, said Joe, had talked to a jeweler in San Antonio who annually cashed the Negro's gold for him.

Joe Brady said that another prospector, by the name of Armstead, told him that the Negro's gold came from a lost mine that was on a fence line southwest of Haystack in a place so brushy that it was extremely hard to see. The way Armstead got into it was that he somehow came by a nugget from this lost mine. He gave the nugget to a friend, an Alpine tourist camp operator by the name of Cooper, as part of a deal by which Cooper grubstaked Armstead in a venture to locate the Lost Haystack Mine and make them both rich. After several days of searching, prospector Armstead was certain of the spot. It was on a fence line southwest of Haystack Mountain, where three or four ranch boundaries cornered together. He had not found an entrance to the mine, but he discovered a telltale air shaft, a sure sign to him that gold was down there in abundance, to be had only for the digging.

But things failed to work out. Armstead could not reach a contract agreement with the three or four ranchers on whose land he would have to dig, and he abandoned hope of getting into the Lost Haystack Mine. The last Joe heard of Armstead, he was making a good living at the carpenter's trade somewhere in New Mexico.

What actually occurred to stir up the prospectors and small-town operators with gold dust in their eyes will never be known. That there was a piece of bull quartz seems incontestable, and men have been known to build dreams of wealth on less than that. Boom towns have risen and fallen on the emptiness of a rumor. For sure, all this Big Bend gossip attracted legend motifs common to many lost mine tales like iron filings to a magnet.

Aside from attaching itself to particular persons and acquiring a legendary map in the process, the story in other versions went on to individualize the mysterious Negro. He grew tall, he grew thin, and he acquired a name. In one version he was a bandit, as Walter Vick of Alpine heard it before 1958 from an uncle. Walter said:

> This story took place in the early 1900s. A gang of outlaws raided around the Sanderson area, and with this gang was one Negro man, who was extra tall and thin. He didn't want to be an outlaw, but society wouldn't accept him, so he decided to join this band for money to go east, where he could be with his own people.
>
> The gang had worked and robbed small places, where not much money was involved. They were not widely known, but the people around in the Big Bend were scared of them.
>
> One morning the gang leader told the Negro of a big gold shipment that should arrive that evening. The holdup was a success, except for one killing. An old man told the outlaws off, and the leader shot him. It made the Negro sick, because he had never seen anyone shoot a helpless old man or anybody else before.
>
> So he grabbed the gold and raced his horse back to camp ahead of the rest. Early in his companionship with the gang, he had found a cave just big enough for him to hide in, and along the way he stopped there and hid the gold. The entrance of this cave was too small for an average man to enter.
>
> Then the Negro and the robbers reached camp at just the same time. Since the leader of the gang never liked the Negro, he shot him for running away like he did. After the Negro died, the rest of the men buried him but never found the gold.
>
> And this story got twisted around from mouth to mouth until finally it became the story of the Lost Negro Mine.

Though the setting of Walter's story is far removed from Haystack Mountain, and though the Negro does not live to make his annual gold pickups, the skinny black man has arrived on the scene of the lost mine legend. Here is the way Harold Page heard it.

> Here near Alpine a Negro man by the name of Mister Johns was riding sheep herd for a rancher. He was of a very slim

build. He weighed somewhere close to one hundred pounds and was close to six foot tall.

One day it was rainy and getting wet and cold. Johns was riding close to the wall of a canyon, and he happened to get off his horse near a crack in the rock. This crack was about a foot wide, and it seemed to go back for some distance.

The tall thin man slid into the wall. The passage went back about fifteen foot and into a small room. This room was about six feet long, six feet wide, and eight or ten feet in height. Johns took a flashlight out of his pocket to look this place over and found the cave to be lined with gold that seemed almost pure. He stayed in the cave until the rain stopped, then went back to his work.

A while later when he was lying on his death bed, he told his grandson where the cave was and what was in it. His grandson, Jim Johns, was a halfbreed, Negro and Indian, with the same skinny build and size of Mister Johns.

The story is told that it took Jim five years to find this mine. When he did, he took an old piece of bedspring and used it for a tool to loosen the gold from the wall. Then he would fill his pockets and leave.

Jim would have the gold changed into money and go to San Antonio. He would stay there until he ran out of money and then come back to get more gold, taking only what he could live on.

One time when he was in San Antonio, a few men tried to make him tell where the gold mine was, but he refused them and they shot him in the stomach. Jim got over this and lived for about a year longer. Then he died of a heart attack.

Just before his death, several men tried to make him tell where the mine was, but they got nothing out of him they didn't already know. Many people have come from all over the United States to look for this gold, but until today this mine is still known as the Lost Mine.

According to Mary Ella Vannoy of Alpine, several of her neighbors remembered seeing the old Negro whose personage became part of these tales. Her Negro is not named or described, and neither does he make his gold pickup in a taxi. She told this story.

In the days when there was much mining and prospecting around Alpine, a Negro man would show up about once a year, take a burro, and go for a camping trip in the mountains. Before long people began to notice that, although he seemed to have very little money before the camping trip, when he returned he would have plenty of money to do anything he wanted.

Naturally people were curious, so one night several of the men in Alpine bought the Negro drinks enough to make him very talkative.They asked him many questions, but they were able to get him to say only that he had found enough riches to last him the rest of his life.

After finding this out, the men tried to follow the Negro on his excursions, but he always managed to lose himself in the mountains. It is believed that the lost mine is somewhere in the vicinity of Haystack Mountain, but in order to get away from his followers, the Negro would sometimes travel as far as Fort Davis before turning back in that direction. When their following the Negro didn't lead them to the mine, many people set out to find it by searching the mountains on their own.

The only man who ever knew the secret of the mine's location was the Negro, and he carried the secret to his death. Ironically, not only the mine's whereabouts is unknown, but the whereabouts of the Negro himself became a mystery. The last time the man was seen—by that time he was quite old—was the day he left on his last burro trip to the mine. When he did not return in several weeks, a search party was formed. Although the burro was found, the old Negro had completely disappeared.

It is said that if the Lost Haystack Mine is ever found, the remains of the lost Negro will be found also.

It is not unlikely that fresh notice of the Lost Haystack Mine will again send goldhunters scrambling over the rocks and through the catclaw brush in search of old fence lines and foot-wide cracks in canyon walls. Not many years ago on a little-used portion of the parking lot at Fritz Weyerts' lumber yard in Alpine, one of Coronado's Children threw up a tall fence and inside it was digging for buried treasure, a burro load or maybe a burro train load of fabulous wealth. The spirit of Midas will never depart.

11.
The Marfa Lights

THE most prolific, on-going legend hatchery in the United States must be the abandoned Marfa airport on Mitchell Flat, the playground of the Marfa Lights.

A favorite pastime in the Big Bend is to drive out at night to see this unexplained phenomenon. When you reach the entrance of the old airport, you park on the shoulder and look south toward the Chinati Mountains about fifty miles away. Against the mountain walls you usually will see one or more of the lights—white, green, or blue; appearing, disappearing; moving diagonally or horizontally. I have seen them myself. Sometimes they seem to approach quite near, as reported by my colleague Mrs. Roy Smith and by many other viewers. On a clear night she and her husband stopped and saw several of the lights near the ground, moving about. The lights would disappear in one spot and reappear in another. Then they seemed to move toward the car and linger near the hood. Getting the creeps by this time, Roy started the engine and headed for home.

During the sixty-odd years Hallie Stillwell has lived in the Big Bend, she has seen such lights many times and in many places. "It looks like a big headlight," she said. "It just kind of flickers along the mountain. They might cover a section or two of land. They light up and run across the mountain, kind of like a grass fire."

In the 1930s Salomón Ramos, then a cowboy working near

Paisano Peak east of Marfa, saw them flickering on the western horizon. In 1927 when Ferdinand Weber observed them in southeastern Presidio County, he was told they were spirits of the Chisos Apaches. In the summer of 1919 cowboys rode all over the mountains to find the source of these lights, without success. About 1900 Roy Stillwell watched them play around the Dead Horse Mountains, in what is now the Big Bend National Park. The earliest reported sighting in 1883, was made by settler Robert Ellison and his wife during their second night in the Big Bend. According to their daughter, Mrs. Lee Plumbley of Marfa, "My daddy said they unloaded their cattle at what is now Alpine and they started driving them toward Marfa. When they came through Paisano Pass and got onto the flats where you can see for a long distance, they saw the light. He thought it was an Apache campfire, and they weren't too friendly in those times. He finally began to realize it wasn't a homeplace or a campfire. Others in the country before him told him they'd always seen it."

Since the folk mind abhors a missing link in the chain of cause and effect, legend is spawned, sometimes disguised as rumor. Mrs. Marie Roberts of Marfa said, "In 1943 during World War II, while working at the Marfa Army Airbase, I overheard two young pilots talking about the strange lights to the south. The boys believed that it was a light used to guide German supply planes in. They were sure that the Germans had a large, well-hidden camp and were getting ready to invade the United States by way of Mexico."

Mrs. Roberts' mother, Mrs. Eva Kerr Jones, said she heard the same tale around 1918: during World War I the light guided German cavalry and pack mules in. Then *her* mother, Mrs. Mary E. Kerr, said that about 1914 the light was said to be Pancho Villa moving in supplies and men, preparing for an all-out attack on the United States. Let it be added that toward the end of World War II it was told that German prisoners at the army airbase were released when Hitler was killed, they headed for Mexico and were never heard from again, and the light is the ghost of Adolf Hitler with a lantern, hunting for his soldiers.

The myth-making goes on, aided especially by students at Sul Ross State University and at the high schools in Marfa and Alpine. Boys like to drive their girls out to the old airbase and get as much scare effect out of the lights as possible. It is all in fun, and they sometimes take along a bottle of cheap wine or a wastebasket full of iced beer. At about third hand, Joan Davis, a Sul Ross student, heard in 1970 that a girl and her date, having gone out to see the lights, were chased by them and knocked down. They hastened home to their dormitories, and next day both discovered they were "sunburned" by the lights. Another student, Buck Reynolds, to intrigue his dates, would start flashing the headlights of his car about a mile before he reached the old airport, as though to call up the lights. When they appeared, he would tell his girl how the lights were "orles" of energy from another planet to monitor the "goings-on" on earth. He would also tell them how his engine once was cut off by the lights. "He would relate these theories," said his interviewer, "with such seeming sincerity that some of his more gullible listeners would be lulled into a nervous shock."

It is said that the airbase was closed because of the deadly lights. During World War II, when the airbase served to train pilots, sometimes the lights would line up like runway lights, and several inexperienced student pilots were killed when these fake guides led them straight into the face of the Chinati Mountain cliffs. That is why the army abandoned the airbase after World War II. Airport officials sent up a helicopter to locate the lights, but they could not be seen from the helicopter. When the men landed where a light was supposed to be, the copter promptly exploded, leaving no trace of the men.

Because of these dubious disasters the U.S. Army seriously set about trying to learn the nature of the Marfa Lights. The most common story, which has several outcomes, tells how during World War II the military organized itself to locate their source. Several jeeps and planes were equipped with intercommunication devices, and the search was on. One jeep was designated to drive directly into a Marfa Light (in the stories the number of men in the jeep is usually given as either two or four). Reports of the outcome of this venture vary:

(1) The jeep reported reaching the light, then contact went dead. The jeep was located, but of its passengers nothing was found except one sock. It was found at a place where the rocks drew heat from the sun, radiated it as light at night, and this burned up the men.

(2) When told they were right on the light, two of the jeep passengers said they saw no light. Then communications broke off. Next day the men were found thrown from the jeep and burned to death. The equipment in the jeep was burned beyond repair.

(3) Two scientists, assigned to help the army, were in the jeep, which was found somewhat melted. The scientists were never found.

An alternate of the version says that two scientists in two trucks were found beside their burning trucks in a state of hysterical shock; both men were idiots from that day on. One person interviewed said, "They sent the two men to a sanitarium in Big Spring. They are supposed to be there up to this date." That was in 1973.

It just might be that the kernel from which all the burned-up jeep stories have sprung has its origin in what C. W. Davis of McCamey told Charles Nichols in 1972. He said, "One of the people involved was a personal friend of mine. He told me that him and two of his buddies were sort of drunk and decided to look for the lights. They stole a jeep, which they wrecked. They were afraid of getting caught, so they set fire to the jeep and sneaked back to the airbase."

Then again, here is what retired postal worker James Mecklin told Gary Painter of Marfa in 1973.

I first came to this country in 1928 to work on a newspaper. As soon as we got here we started hearing about the Marfa Lights. We saw the lights several times and spent a week trying to find them. Later on when World War II came along I was in charge of the post office at the airbase. One morning I was talking to a Sergeant Robarbe was his name, he was a mail orderly, and he was from New York and all he knew was pavement and he thought these antelope were funny looking cows, things like that you know. Anyway we got to talking about this light, and, boy, that intrigued him a whole lot and some way or another he got to talking to his squadron commander, a Major Davidson, and he was interested in the stars, astronomy. He was an amateur astronomer. So, boy, he comes hot foot'n it down there and wants me to tell him about these lights.

About a week and he was already het up about it. He'd been out there every night seeing it, and there'd been some talk and he got to listening and they wondered if it was cars or something over there or what.

But me telling him about it, that was what impressed him there was maybe something strange. He investigated and got his maps out and looked at this highway. They had maps of all this country drawn up by the base, and he couldn't locate any ranch houses or anything that would make this light. So he thought maybe, well, there is something out there.

So he asked me, said "Do you think that we could follow that thing by an airplane?"

So I said, "Well I don't know if you could follow it by an airplane or not."

He sad, "We got a lot of 'em out here."

They were flying these old twin-engine Cessnas made out of plywood, mostly to train in school there. Those twin-engines, they were death traps.

He said, "Well, I can get hold of some planes." Says, "You know, I'm going to check this thing out." Says, "I'm tired of all this stuff I've heard about this."

Meanwhile he talked to other people in Marfa and got the same ideas about the light as he got from me and heard a bunch of stories about it and said, "We're going to put an end to all this. We're going to check it out."

I wasn't in on this, but they told me that for three nights he set up teams out there of four planes, one behind the other, and that they would follow that light. When they took off they could see it come and go. After they got to where they thought it was, it would disappear. Then maybe it would appear way down ahead of them, and pretty soon it was ending up in Mexico, where they couldn't go. It moved ahead of them all the time. It would disappear on them, then pick up and go.

This man finally gave up on it, this Major Davidson, and he was mystified. The last time I talked to him before he left, he said, "Mecklin, I'm leaving you and Marfa and your light here. I'd sure like to have found out what it was but couldn't do it."

A man who actually flew in hope of finding the nature of the light was Fritz Kahl of Marfa. He runs a flying service today at the old airbase and some years ago organized the International Soaring Contest there. He told his interviewer, "What I have to tell you, I could say in five minutes. I chased them in an airplane, not once but several times, and this was in 1943 and early 1944. My God, there I was, a World War II aviator. Hell, I was twenty-one years old and didn't have any sense, flying airplanes at night out in the hills, right down on the ground. You got to be young. You got to be crazy. But we tried it. Only thing is, you know, you leave the airbase and you get out on that Presidio highway a ways, and you run into the hills right quick." Fritz Kahl could find nothing.

Stories that grew out of these airborne quests claimed that they dropped sacks of flour to mark the location of the lights, then next day could find nothing but flour. Sometimes not even flour.

In general, there are two or three sets of legends about the Marfa Lights, and the nature of each set depends upon which generation of the folk it serves, the older or the younger.

The older folk might be served well by what Mrs. W. T. Giddens, who was raised in the Chinatis, told "Off the Beaten Trail" columnist Ed Syers. Of a tradition in her family, she said, "I've seen the Ghost Lights all my life and can't remember their causing any harm other than fright. They like to follow you out in the pasture at night, seem to be drawn to people and stock, and animals don't seem to fear them at all." Then Mrs. Giddens told about her father, lost at night in a blizzard miles from home. He thought he would freeze to death when he saw the Marfa Lights flashing almost on him. They "said" to him (he could never explain how) that he was three miles south of Chinati Peak, off his trail, heading in the wrong direction. They "told" him he would die if he didn't follow the lights, which he did. They led him to a small cave, and in that shelter he lived through the night, the largest of lights staying close beside him. Somehow he was "told" they were spirits from long before that wanted to save him, and that he could sleep now without freezing to death. With morning both the lights and the blizzard were gone. And as anticipated, he saw that he was off the trail, three miles south of Chinati. Then getting home was no chore at all.

This family tradition spawned further, more simplified legends. A cowboy was lost in a blizzard at night at the foot of the Chinatis. A ghost light appeared and at first he tried to get away from it, but it followed him. Changing his mind, he followed the light for hours, and it made him feel comfortable somehow. When the light suddenly disappeared, the cowboy was happy to find that it had led him to one of the Presidio County Airport gates. Then he followed the road home to Marfa.

The Marfa Lights are friendly in other tales also. They are the ghost of a rancher who once owned the land, and they always shine brighter on his birthday. Another tradition says that early settlers used the Marfa Lights as a guide across Mitchell Flat to avoid encounter with hostile Indians.

Some of the older legends tell of Indians, a subject frequently present in American myth made early in this century. Several of these are pseudo Indian legends, a few having to do with the stars. For instance, the lights are temporary homes of fallen stars, and the Great Spirit stores his thunderbolts with them. As the fire in the stars goes out, they die, and as they have served the Great Spirit well as sentries, he allows them to choose their final resting place. Some of the stars are Apache warriors who fought bravely against the white man, and they have been granted their request to come back to the land they love.

Some say the lights are ghosts of Indians. Once Indians were camped on the flat, on their way to plunder in Mexico. Soldiers from Fort Davis attacked and annihilated most of them. Seeking venegeance, survivors stole lanterns from the settlers and moved around at night, hoping to lure the soldiers into a trap. Their ghosts wave their deceptive lanterns to this day. Another version says that all these Indians were killed in camp, except their scout, and he still wanders with his Ghost Light trying to find his people. In another tale the Indians were not killed but captured when their chief was absent, and they were carted off to a reservation in Florida. It is their chief who continues the ghostly search. Or, according to another tale, it was the chief that was killed, and the tribesmen are looking for him.

Spaniards get the blame for rounding up Indians into slavery and then cutting off the chief's head. To their astonishment, the chief picked up his head and walked away with a lantern to find his tribesmen. He got other chiefs to join him, and all those lights are the Indian chiefs searching for their captive fellows.

Some of these stories about the ghost of an Indian chief are tied in with the once very real Chisos Apache chief Alsate. History says that he and his tribe were betrayed at San Carlos, Mexico, and enslaved; legend says that after he escaped, he returned to the Chisos to live with his wife. Alternate legend holds that he was camped with his Apaches in the Chinati Mountains and that the Spaniards were determined to massacre the lot. They invited Alsate and his tribe to their camp to talk peace, only to ambush them. Alsate escaped to the Chinatis, and his spirit is still lighting fires to summon his dead warriors back to his camp.

Inevitably pseudo Indian legends turn to the love between a handsome Brave and a beautiful Indian Princess. A story apparently designed to entertain children is one Betty Burns said she was told by her mother. An Indian Princess and a Brave were in love. Each evening they brought separate herds of sheep down from the Chinatis. Once while she was waiting for him, she saw a flash of light. When he did not join her, she searched for him but found only his belt around the neck of one of his sheep. Where the light had appeared, the ground was disturbed. Though she had many suitors, she vowed never to marry but continued to search for her beloved. Finally only one suitor was left. Every week on the day her Brave disappeared, the light would appear, and one day, when she approached too close, she was blinded by the light. Then the tribe moved away, leaving only the Princess and her lone suitor. Though blind, she went again to find her lover. Her suitor found her dead next day at the bottom of a cliff. Her loyal suitor lived on at that place and believed that the light dancing around was the spirit of the blind Princess still searching for her handsome Brave.

Alsate gets into one story of this kind, according to which he fell in love with an Indian girl and a jealous suitor plotted to kill him. When the jealous suitor followed Alsate and the girl to their trysting place, he accidentally killed the girl instead of Alsate. Then he stole her body and hid it in the mountains. The lights, then, are Alsate and the girl searching for each other.

In another account a Brave had gone for water when enemy Indians killed all the tribe except the girl he loved, and she had disappeared. With the Marfa Lights, he is still looking for his sweetheart. A tangent story says that the light is an Indian searching for his slain sweetheart, and that he turns off the light when he thinks someone is watching him.

A love interest also is the central element in the story of the Indian chief whose daughter ran away to Mexico with a man of whom he did not approve. The chief is still burning these lights so that his daughter can find her way home. Another Indian chief went looking for the girl he loved and could not find her. As the tale teller put it, "He set himself on fire because he was so upset." And that is an explanation of the Marfa Lights.

There are many stories about Indians using the lights to hunt for somebody or something. A chief awoke one morning to find that every person in his tribe had vanished; to find his lost tribe his spirit is still wandering with a lantern. A chief was killed, and it is his son searching for his grave with a light. An Indian chief was killed by white men and buried in a manner unholy to the Indians; he wanders about with a ghost lantern searching for his soul so that he can enter the Happy Hunting Ground.

One pseudo Indian story connects the lights with buried treasure. Gold is said to be hidden in a sacred Indian burial ground, which was not to be desecrated. One night several drunk Indians went in to find the gold and never returned. The Marfa Lights are those Indians trying to find their way out.

Or the lights are forms taken by an Indian, his wife, and their descendants. When he died, he became a bright light, then so did his wife, and then his children after them. When visitors intrude on their land the lights are this Indian family performing a war-dance.

A story with a particular Mexican-American and Catholic bent says that once two warring tribes fought a battle in which nearly all were killed. The Marfa Lights are the spirits of these Indians walking the earth in penance.

Another tale says that an Indian and his wife rode into Marfa for supplies. While the Indian was at the store, a white man tried to rape the Indian woman and she shot him dead. When the Indian saw what had happened, to protect his wife he took the gun in his own hand and told her to run and hide.

He was caught, did not deny the murder charge, and was hanged on the spot. Every night his wife—now a ghost—burns a fire to signal him to return.

Similar is a more recent story about a woman who got sick when she was traveling with her husband in the mountains. The husband went to town to bring a doctor but, nobody knows why, never returned. The sick lady, now presumably dead, keeps shining a light so he can find her.

Sometimes the stories borrow from the Dolores legend. In the 1800s a Ranger and his wife lived in the hills between Marfa and Alpine. Being a lawman, he usually was away from home at night. His wife had a lover, and she would signal her friend that the coast was clear by climbing a mountain and starting a fire. The lover also would start a fire, to let her know he was on his way to join her. After a year the woman's lover did not respond one night, and for about two weeks she saw no answering blaze. Then she learned that her husband had killed her amorous friend. After that, in her lover's honor, she would go up the mountain every night and start her fire. Her ghost is still making the Marfa Lights.

The story of an Indian tribe in the Chinatis that was struck by famine combines both the Dolores and Llorona motifs (La Llorona is the ghost that wanders and wails in penance for drowning her babies). When the famine was at its worst, an Indian woman gave birth to twins. Worried about their survival, she summoned the devil, pleaded for his help, and agreed to turn her children over to him when they were older. According to contract, the devil provided them always with food, good health, shelter, and clothing. Now the lights are this old Indian woman "searching and signaling for her twins to come back to her from the devil." So it is told by Mrs. Conaly Brooks, who grew up in Marfa.

A Llorona type also figures in what Jesús Jacquez told Ysrael Valencia had happened to him. Jesús was a trapper in the Marfa and Chinati area. When returning at night from working their traps, he and his fellow trappers would see lights flashing against the cliffs. "Then we would see a woman up ahead of us," he said, "signaling for us to follow her into the mountains, where the lights had been flashing. The first time we saw her, we thought she needed help. We tried to call her, but she always started walking back and would wave for us to follow her. Of course no one had the nerve to do that. Every time we made those trapping trips, we always saw the same lights and the same woman." Doing a little myth-patching of his own, Valencia said maybe she was the ghost of an Indian woman trying to get help for those Indians wounded in the Mexican ambush.

Some of the older stories relate the lights to rustlers, outlaws, and lawmen. In pioneer days an outlaw killed a woman, who was the sheriff's wife. The sheriff and a posse went hunting for the murderer, and when they reached the mountains, the food ran out. The posse gave up and went home, but the sheriff stayed at it and is still wandering the Chinatis with his ghost light, seeking revenge. Then there was the cowboy who turned bad and was rustling cattle from his own boss' outfit. One night he saw the lights flashing about, took them to be a warning from God, and went straight from that day onward.

A Mexican-American father put the Marfa Lights to disciplinary use. When his son grew curious about the lights, he told the boy they were campfires of smugglers and rustlers who would kill him if he started snooping around.

Beau White of Marfa said his grandfather told him about a rancher who lived in the Davis Mountains in the 1850s and had become rather wealthy. One day while he was working on the range, Mexican bandits plundered and burned his house and barns. They raped the man's wife and twenty-year-old daughter, forcing his two younger sons to watch. Then the bandits bound the whole family with wet rawhide around their throats and wrists and left them to die. When the rancher returned, what he found drove him insane. Taking the lantern the Mexicans used to set fire to his property, he mounted his horse and went in pursuit. By this time the bandits had escaped to a place south of Marfa, had buried their loot on Mitchell Flat, and were headed for Mexico with plans to return and pick up their money. That night they hid out in a cave in the Chinatis and were sleeping when the rancher found them. The rancher built a fire at the cave entrance, and when the bandits came out, he shot them in the legs. Then he dragged them back into the cave and burned them alive. The rancher was never heard of again. The Marfa Lights are the Mexicans coming back in search of their hidden loot, and also the rancher looking for his money with the lantern.

Other pioneer stories abound. A wagon train was camped and destroyed by Indians. The Marfa Lights are the wagon train's ghost campfires. Once an old man went through west Texas cutting down all the trees. Near Marfa he chopped down a huge oak that fell on him and killed him. When he was found, his arms and legs were missing. The Marfa Lights are this old axeman's arms and legs seeking to rejoin his body.

They are also believed to be the ghosts of Shafter miners killed in a cave-in, the ghosts of buffalo, and the spirit of a negligent soldier who fell asleep while on guard at a fort in the Marfa area. Indians attacked and killed everybody, and the soldier's spirit cannot rest because he did not do his duty.

The Marfa Lights stories readily connect with tales of buried treasure, almost all of which are in Mexican-American oral tradition. To begin with, all treasures are guarded by mysterious lights. In the days of Spanish occupation, there was a gold mine near San Carlos, Mexico. The Spaniards, after forcing the Indians to carry gold to the Marfa area and dig, killed the Indians and buried them with the gold. Those Indian spirits rise and dance above the treasure, and they say, "If you can find the exact spot of the light, dig and you will find the gold."

A family tradition, said Mrs. Olga Parraz of Marfa, tells of an attempt by her husband's father, brother, and two uncles to find a treasure that was hidden by Indians to keep it from the Spaniards. In their car the men followed the light over rough country, and when they got close, they started digging. Suddenly, out of nowhere, a very old car appeared beside them. Frightened, they ran back to their own car and gave up the treasure hunt forever.

In another tale two men were digging for gold and were about to dig up a treasure of Indian coins. Their blood ran cold when they heard a voice say, "I am the chief of the Indians and I am supposed to take care of the gold." This shows that the Marfa Lights are the souls of Indians protecting the gold so that nobody will take it.

Or the lights are reflections of gems in a treasure buried by a settler from the north. He wanted to marry an Indian girl, but her father, the chief, refused to unite her to a white man. When the settler offered countless priceless jewels in trade, however, the chief changed his mind. The white man went away to find enough gems, and when he returned the tribe had been wiped out by enemy Indians. He found his sweetheart's grave and buried the jewels with her. Hence, the Marfa Lights.

An Anglo-American treasure tale says that on one of the mountains is a red handprint, which can be seen but is impossible to reach. The hand points to a grove of cottonwood trees planted in the shape of a horseshoe, though this pattern is obliterated by later growth. The Indians hid their gold in the center of the horseshoe, and the Marfa Lights are Indian spirits guarding that gold.

They say, too, that an old prospector who had heard of gold deposits between Marfa and Alpine roamed Mitchell Flat and the Chinatis for seven years. He kept a map, and each night by the light of his campfire, he marked with a circle the place he had dug that day. The Marfa Lights are the ghosts of his many campfires.

Stories of more recent vintage move from the horse-and-buggy days to our motorized era. Besides being the ghosts of airmen killed in crashes at the old army airbase, the lights are reputed to be the ghosts of people killed in civilian planes. One tale says a pilot was flying seven passengers to their home near Del Rio. In rough weather and almost out of gas, he decided to land on what looked like a lighted runway. What he saw was some sort of reflection off the mountainside, and he crashed into the cliff. Supposedly the lights emanate from that dead pilot trying to locate his seven passengers.

Sometimes they are responsible for fatal carwrecks: the lights shoot out in front of cars, blind the driver, and thus have caused several head-on collisions. Once some out-of-state travelers on Highway 90 saw what seemed to be reflectors on the side of the road. When their car was found, the interior was burned to ashes, and the only remains were nonflammable objects such as coins, keys, and jewelry. The outside of the car was unharmed.

Many stories involving cars and jeeps are the result of young people trying to impress each other with hair-raising tales. A boy and a girl were parked on the old airbase when they saw the lights. The girl began to scream with fright and the boy started the car. As they were leaving, the lights gained on them and the back of the car got hot. The back tires blew out, and the couple ran to safety. Next day the car was melted and still smoking hot. In another version of this same story, the girl died of shock. About a week later the boy went back to the scene of the accident and was never seen again.

Local high-school students went out in a jeep to see the lights and did not return. Searchers followed the tire tracks to where they abruptly stopped in an arroyo, but no further trace was ever found. The lights are those vanished young people signaling with ghost-jeep headlights, still hoping to be rescued.

Countless stories, usually very much alike, tell of young people going out to see the lights, being frightened by their approach, then hastening back home or to the dormitory. Some of the stories, always at least third or fourth hand, mention damage done by the lights. For example: a driver going west on Highway 90 was pursued by a light ten feet tall. At a hundred miles per hour, he could not outrun it, but finally it disappeared. When he reached the bridge on the edge of Marfa, he found that the right back side of his car was burned black.

Always there have been a host of explanations that attribute natural causes to the Marfa Lights. One of the oldest is that they are sotol burned by cowboys to light their camp or to mark their trail.

With the younger generation, myth and science merge. Hundreds of years ago, Mitchell Flat was an ocean bed, and there was a lighthouse that is still signaling to ghost ships. Or, the ghosts of the sailors are out there signaling with the lights for the ships to pick them up.

Numerous "scientific" explanations have been advanced.

Mica
Gasses from the ground
Uranium
Mercury vapor lamps on ranches (strenuously denied by old-timers)
Bat guano in caves
Little volcanoes
Reflection of the stars and moon off rocks
Swamp gas
Phosphorus in the rocks
Phosphorus buried by phosphorus hunters
Chemicals left by the army at the old airport
Reflections from silver left in the abandoned Shafter mines
Coal deposits
Bones in the earth
Static electricity
Irregular "pockets" in the air that collect light, analogous to the telephoto lens
Reflections from a comet or meteor
Water flowing between two different ores, which gives off static electricity

Gas formed into large balls, which are somehow ignited

A negative charge, which if it ever met a positive charge would blow up the earth

Jack rabbits, whose fur glows because they have run through luminescent brush or have picked up glowworms.

The appeal of the unknown in these lights is strong enough to arouse sensible men to elaborate and expensive investigative action in their determination to conquer the mystery of the Marfa Lights and lay bare their natural disposition. This appeal is as strong as the tug of treasure maps handed down by dying prisoners to Coronado's Children, sending them into the wilderness with canteens and shovels and hearts full of yearning. Periodically at Sul Ross State University some young professor or student organizes a Marfa Light Investigation Expedition. Like the name of Fritz Kahl, their names live on in the legends: Paul Moran, Ring Huggins, Bill Juraschek, Ron Reynolds, and Don Witt. They load themselves with surveying equipment, they triangulate the lights, they level on them with high-powered binoculars, they walkie-talkie back and forth from planes and pick-ups, they coordinate observations with radio-equipped cars, and they continue to drop sacks of flour despite all the former flour-sack failures. In freezing cold and dark of early spring, 1975, an expedition set out. The Sul Ross *Skyline* reported, "Utilizing aircraft, survey instruments, multiband radio equipment, and about half a dozen search teams, the Marfa Ghost Light hunt began about 9:30 P.M. More than a hundred carloads of observers gathered between the two observation points, one at Paisano Pass and the other at the entrance to the old Presidio County Airport. Homer Hime, Alpine High School math instructor, and Don Witt were stationed at Paisano Pass, where Witt was to direct a team of observers in an airplane flown by Fritz Kahl. Hime was to keep in touch with ground crews stationed at various points on the flat plains between Paisano Pass and the Chinati

Mountains. But mixup in schedules sent the airplane aloft at 8:30 P.M. rather than the scheduled 9:30 P.M., and the search was called off a little after 11:00 P.M." With a prospector's unconquerable spirit, Witt said, "We'll begin the search at 9:30 tomorrow night and follow the same procedure."

Finally, there are the super-science and UFO stories of quite recent date, though some perhaps go back to World War II. One story says that between 1942 and 1945, the United States government built experiment stations throughout the Southwest to develop secret weapons. These were at Los Alamos, White Sands, and the Chinati Mountains Research Center, all secret and in remote desert areas. To work in these places, the government brought in the best of the world's scientists. The atomic bomb was developed at Los Alamos and missiles at White Sands, but at the Chinati Center, the most secret project of all proved a failure. An M.I.T. nuclear physicist, originally from Israel, was working on a nuclear laser fusion device. The project failed because it was years ahead of its time and created extremely dangerous risks. When a test in the field ran into trouble, the light generated by the laser interfered with the foreign fringes of matter. This caused the laser-fusion light to be locked or lost in space and time. A gigantic explosion followed, which destroyed the research center and left a seven-mile-wide scorch area. The accident was kept secret, but the government sent special investigative teams to study the strange flashes known as the Marfa Lights. After their investigation, they considered the matter closed and refused to give any information. This story, told by Ray Fuller of Marfa to Ellis Villalobos, was said to come from Ray's "Aunt Mary" of Marfa.

Some recent explanations enter into the realm of unidentified flying objects and the fourth dimension. In Indian times a flying saucer from outer space landed. The ship and its occupants were invisible except for their lights. Then again, on the old airbase there is an invisible barrier to that other dimension which keeps opening in spots, and that is what makes the

lights. People who have disappeared out there are still in limbo
in the fourth dimension. It is said that a well-informed science
writer once camped for many weeks to study the lights. He
formed a theory, and "his recorded theory was so controversial
that the government confiscated it."

Keeping pace with developments in our national culture,
perhaps the most recent tale deals with a young Jesus Freak
who went out to the old airbase with other students. Whenever
he would say anything about Jesus, the lights would appear;
when the subject changed, they would fade out.

A failure of the Marfa Lights to appear was described by
Vickie Smith in 1972. She told her friends about the lights, the
burned-up jeep, the disappearing passengers, the flour bom-
bardments, the lost Indians. She threw in a few stories of her
own about people who went to see the lights, after which only
parts of their bodies were found, burned and scattered about.
Then Vickie and her crowd jumped in the car, drove out, and
parked on the highway by Mitchell Flat to see the mysterious
performers.

No lights. They waited. Still no lights. Vickie's friends
grumbled their disbelief.

As they were about to give up and go home, a huge school
bus pulled off the highway and about thirty-five children
swarmed out of it. They were yelling "I wanna see the Marfa
Lights, man, where are they? 'Cause we're gonna find out what
they are."

Their teacher, who was driving the bus, asked Vickie if
this was the place they were supposed to see the Marfa Lights.
He said he brought this busload of pupils from the Texas Pan-
handle on a tour to include the lights and then started telling
scores of yarns he had heard about them. Riding back to Alpine, Vickie said to her friends, "I told you I wouldn't lie about
a thing like that."

Notes on Sources

1.
The Devil in the Big Bend

Informants for this chapter were Ralph Sigala of Del Rio (who unearthed in Alpine a typescript in Spanish entitled "Un Paseo a la Montaña de la Cruz," signed by C. Bowles, Pastor, and dated December 10, 1925); from Alpine, Mrs. B. F. Berkeley, Miss Isabel Lafarelle, Mrs. Berta Lassiter, Mrs. Ethel Nail, Miss Grace Segura, Mr. Milton Smith, Mr. V. J. Smith, Mrs. Kathryn Walker, and my wife, Lillian, who obtained stories from Mrs. Carmen Lafarelle; and Señor Jesús Ronana and Señor Nieves Samaniego of Ojinaga, Mexico. The photographs that apply to this chapter were taken by Glenn Burgess, now living in Safford, Arizona. New material has been combined with information contained in an essay by Mody C. Boatright, "The Devil's Grotto," in *Texas and Southwestern Lore*, ed. J. Frank Dobie, Texas Folklore Society Publication no. 6 (Austin, 1927), pp. 102–106.

2.
Christ in the Big Bend

Sources for these stories are many, and I remember especially those stories told by Petra Valenzuela, Kate Davis, and Ester Gonzales about 1951. Ted Sánchez wrote "Nuestro Padre Jesus" for *Sage* (Fall, 1950), the student literary magazine at Sul Ross State University. In 1972 Joe Valenzuela transcribed what was told to him by Carolina P. Molinar and in 1973 Russell J. Gardenier of Presidio put together what he obtained from many sources. These papers are in the Folklore Collection of the English Department at Sul Ross State University.

3.

Chisos Ghosts

The earliest reference to the mountains as Los Chisos is that of Captain Don Juan Bautista Elguézabel in a report to Jacabo Ugarte, Presidio del Norte, April 21, 1787, translated by Al B. Nelson in "Campaigning in the Big Bend of the Rio Grande in 1787," *Southwestern Historical Quarterly* 39 (January, 1936): 213 (the Sierra del Carmen, also mentioned, is the next range to the east of Los Chisos, extending well into Mexico). M. W. T. Chandler's reference to Los Chisos is in his report to William H. Emory, *Report of the United States and Mexican Boundary Survey* (Washington, D.C., 1857), 1: 83, and Robert T. Hill's is in "Running the Canyons of the Rio Grande," *Century* 61 (January, 1901): 381.

Presidio High School's Spanish teacher, Miss Eva Nieto, always heard that *los Chisos* comes from *hechizo*, "charming." In a speech in the Big Bend National Park, a Mexican government official once emphasized this etymology. When I first encountered Walter Fulcher's doubts about this folk meaning, they were in manuscript form. Now they are in print in *The Way I Heard It: Tales of the Big Bend*, ed. Elton Miles (Austin: The University of Texas Press, 1959), pp. 41–46. Upon inquiry by letter, Apache-language expert Harry Hoijer of the University of California supplied his views in a reply, November 1, 1956.

Information about the Chisos Apaches and their name for themselves is put together from various sources: Vito Alessio Robles, *Coahuila y Texas en la Epoca Colonial* (México, D.F.: Editorial Cultura, 1938), p. 39; a letter to me from José Carlos Chávez of Chihuahua, April 17, 1957, translated by M. P. Slover, Alpine; Lope de Sierra Osorio, who wrote, "The other nations lately in rebellion . . . have different names such as Chizos, Julimes, and others which it is impossible to remember, included under the appellation of Conchos, which is the more general name," in Charles Wilson Hackett, *Historical Documents Relating to New Mexico, Nueva Vizcaya, and Approaches Thereto, to 1773* (Washington, D.C.: The Carnegie Institute, 1926), 2: 221.

Not until this study was under way was the placing of the Chisos in the Athapascan language family seriously considered, as anthropologists seem to have followed the precedent set by Lope de Sierra Osorio in 1685. For example, John R. Swanton's classification in *The Indian Tribes of North America*, Smithsonian Institution, Bureau of American Ethnology Bulletin no. 145 (Washington, D.C.:

The Government Printing Office, 1953), p. 619, is based on that of
J. Alden Mason, "The Native Languages of Middle America," and
of Frederick Johnson, "The Linguistic Map of Mexico and Central
America," in *The Mayas and Their Neighbors*, ed. William B. Max-
well (New York: Appleton-Century, 1940), pp. 52–87, 88–114.
Mason wrote to me in a letter, March 22, 1957, that his study relied
heavily on Carl Sauer, *The Distribution of Aboriginal Tribes and
Languages in Northwestern Mexico* (Ibero-Americana: 5 [Berkeley:
University of California Press, 1934]), p. 63, where Sauer says,
"The slender evidence that we have is that they [the Chiso] were
a part of the Concho." [Sauer's evidence is contained in the so-
called Parral documents, which is Hackett's *Historical Documents*,
and apparently is Osorio's statement above.] Before Sauer's study,
says Mason, the region "immediately south of the Rio Grande" was
"formerly ascribed to the Apache" [see Mason, "The Native Languages," p. 69.], but the Chisos should be classified as Athapascan
in language.

Some historical data about the Chisos Apaches is put together
from Hackett, *Historical Documents*, 2: 211, 219, 221, 335, 397;
from the Chávez letter of April 17, 1957, which cites *Documentos
para la Historia de México* (Mexico, D.F., 1857), 4: 146, 147, 160,
and Nicolás de Lafora, *Relación del viaje que hizo a los Presidios
Internos situados en la frontera de la América septentrional pertene-
ciente al Rey de España*, ed. P. Robredo (Mexico, D.F., 1939);
and from O. W. Williams, *Alsate: The Last of the Chisos Apaches*
(pamphlet published at Fort Stockton, Texas, n.d.)

Names for the Apache and the Chisos and their pronunciations
are supported in Frederick Webb Hodge (ed.), *Handbook of American Indians* (Washington, D.C., n.d.), 1: 67, 285, 846, and by
Mrs. Andree F. Sjoberg, ethnographer of Austin, Texas, who wrote
to me on February 16, 1957, that "an old book entitled *A Vocabulary of the Navaho Language* (Franciscan Fathers) gives *chishi* as
a Navaho word for the Chiricahua Apache." Swanton (*Indian
Tribes*, p. 328) lists the Laguna names for the Apache as *chishye*
and *tshishe*. It is Harry Hoijer who told me that *chishi* is said to
mean "people of the forest," (letter, November 1, 1956).

Individual informants for folktales about Chisos ghosts are
mentioned in the text. Walter Fulcher's tales are in *The Way I
Heard It*, pp. 41–46.

Traditions related to Chisos ghosts include the place name El
Cerro del Hechicero Quemado ("The Hill of the Burned Witch"),
designating a mountain in Mexico south of the Chisos Mountains.

For more about La Llorona, see Soledad Pérez, "The Weeping Woman," in *The Healer of Los Olmos*, ed. Wilson M. Hudson, Texas Folklore Society Publication no. 24 (Dallas, Texas: The Southern Methodist University Press, 1941), pp. 73–76. Recently, La Llorona has developed the habit of conducting her terrifying search at city dumps of West Texas towns where there are no running streams.

The story about the Indian mother's fear that her baby might turn into an animal may be more Spanish and Mexican in origin than Apachean. In Dallas on April 12, 1957, Dr. Walter Starkie, then of the British Institute in Madrid, told me, "Spanish Gypsies are terrified by the moon. They believe that a baby born in the moonlight may turn into some sort of animal."

4.

Old Fort Leaton

A search covering many years for information on Ben Leaton and the Leaton-Burgess feud was virtually completed by essential missing links from oral tradition supplied by Mrs. Corrinne Cage and Mrs. Helen Adams of Presidio, Texas, and by Mrs. Hope Tarwater of La Mula, Mexico. Their details added much to information gathered from Carlysle Graham Raht, *The Romance of the Davis Mountains and Big Bend Country* (El Paso: The Rahtbooks Co., 1919) and other printed and oral sources. In *Baronial Forts of the Big Bend* (San Antonio: Trinity University Press, 1967), Leavitt Corning, Jr., cites documents which set straight many facts that had become distorted in the local tales about Fort Leaton. It is established, for instance, that the Juana Pedrosa of the tales was in reality Juana Pedraza.

Ben Leaton and "his brother" were identified as "old Apache traders" from Tennessee in John Henry Brown's account of the Jack Hays visit ("The 'Chihuahua–El Paso' Pioneer Expedition in 1848," in L. E. Daniell *Indian Wars and Pioneers of Texas* [Austin, Texas, n.d.], pp. 104–105). Brown knew these men and says the name is pronounced "Layton." Disparaging allusions to "traders on the frontiers of Texas" in 1850 came from Annie Heloise Abel (ed.), *The Official Correspondence of James S. Calhoun While Indian Agent at Santa Fe and Superintendent of Indian Affairs in New Mexico*, (Washington, D.C.: Government Printing Office, 1915), pp. 51–52, 108–109. Josiah Gregg calls Ben Leaton "a desperado" in Maurice Garland Fulton (ed.), *Diary and Letters of Josiah Gregg* (Norman: University of Oklahoma Press, 1944), 2: 127. Information about the

Traders Company in the Mexican War is from William E. Connel-ley, *Doniphan's Expedition* (Topeka, Kansas, 1907). The new route to Chihuahua from San Antonio, known as the Chihuahua Trail, was often traveled in the 1880s and 1890s by August Santleben, author of *A Texas Pioneer*, ed. I. D. Affleck (New York: Neale Publishing Co., 1910).

I am indebted to Jerry Sullivan of the Texas State Parks and Wildlife Commission for showing me documentary evidence that Ben Leaton was one of John Johnson's scalp hunters and was pres-ent at the Santa Rita Massacre in New Mexico. He is so listed in the May 5, 1837, issue of *El Noticioso de Chihuahua*, which reported the massacre as having occurred on April 22 (*Periódico Oficial de Chihuahua*, microfilm roll 1, frames 460–462, University of Texas at El Paso). Leaton is so identified also in another Mexican docu-ment, of April 24, 1837, translated in William C. McGaw, *Savage Scene: The Life and Times of James Kirker, Frontier King* (New York: Hastings House Publishers, 1972), pp. 110–111. It is Jerry Sullivan who established the fact that Leaton died in San Antonio about August 1, 1851, give or take a few days.

The story about Leaton's harem comes from Owen P. White, *Texas: An Informal Biography* (New York: G. P. Putnam's Sons, 1945), p. 136. The death of young Burgess is recorded in John E. Gregg, "History of Presidio County" (master's thesis, University of Texas; printed in the 1936 Centennial Edition of *Voice of the Mex-ican Border*, an excellent but short-lived magazine published in Marfa by Mrs. Jack Shipman). The description of Fort Leaton and Presidio del Norte by William Henry Chase Whiting is contained in Ralph P. Bieber (ed.), *Exploring Southwestern Trails, 1946–1954* (Glendale, California: The Arthur H. Clark Co., 1938).

About Ed Hall—was he Benjamin Leaton's half brother or stepbrother? Mrs. Tarwater says that some old-timers in Presidio claim that there was no Ben Leaton, rather that the *jefe* of the old fort was named Ed Leaton. John Henry Brown says Ben Leaton had a brother but does not tell his name. Ed Hall appears as Juana Leaton's new husband in Mrs. O. L. and Jack Shipman, "The Savage Saga," in *Voice of the Mexican Border* (1938), pp. 6–13. "The Savage Saga" contains some details of the feud, as does James Leaverton and Kathleen Houston, "Presidio County's Oldest Build-ing, Fort Leaton," in *Voice of the Mexican Border* (Centennial Edi-tion, 1936), pp. 85–86.

A Mexican version of the murder of John Burgess does not in-volve the Negro. According to Mrs. Marguerite Madrid of Redford,

Texas, Burgess went to the general store in Fort Davis for supplies, and after he started home he remembered an item he had forgotten to buy. Upon reentering the store, he met Bill Leaton, who shot him down. Like many Mexican tales, this one concludes with a moral: "So you see, if he hadn't forgotten something, things would have turned out different."

Family-tradition stories told by Juan Burgess and Victor Leaton Ochoa are in the Shipman Collection, File no. 1, "Fort Leaton," Sul Ross State University English Department Folklore Collection, Helen Adams Papers. This file includes copies of the feature on Juan Leaton by Mrs. Jack Shipman in 1922 for the El Paso *Herald* and the reply to it by Victor Leaton Ochoa as told to G. A. Martin, ("Victor Leaton Ochoa," El Paso *Herald*, November 11, 1922). Still more variant family tales were collected by Mabel Lowry from Joseph Larkin Burgess and Joseph Larkin Burgess, Jr., in Huntington Beach, California, and from Edward Nieto of Presidio, Texas. She sets them forth in "Fort Leaton State Historic Park, Presidio County, Texas," the 1969 report she prepared for the Park Services Division of the Texas Parks and Wildlife Department, Austin, Texas.

As for the ages of the persons involved, oral tradition says that William Leaton was eighteen years old when he killed John Burgess in 1875. Also, the cemetery at Fort Leaton once contained a large headstone on which was engraved:

BURGESS
John D.
1820–1875
Tomasita
1835–1876

The last time I was there, it was gone. Two other graves are marked "John B. Burgess, Aug. 15, 1853–Feb. 15, 1927" and "Paz L. Burgess, Jan. 24, 1856–Feb. 12, 1929." Another grave, covered by a concrete slab and enclosed by an iron fence, is unmarked, save for a rickety wooden cross.

5.

Water Witching in the Big Bend

One of the studies that tried to bring scientific analysis to water witching was that of Sir William Barrett and Theodore Besterman, *The Divining Rod: An Experimental and Scientific Investigation* (London: Methuen & Co., 1926). For medieval origins of modern dowsing, see Herbert Clark Hoover and Lou Henry (trans.) *Agricola: De Re Metallica* (New York: Dover Publications, 1950), pp. 38–41. Varieties of superstition attached by the folk to dowsing are described in Sir James Frazier, *The Golden Bough*, vol. 2, *Balder the Beautiful* (New York: MacMillan & Co., 1955), pp. 67–69, 281–282; and also in *The Encyclopedia of Religion and Ethics* (New York: Charles Scribner's Sons, 1955), s.v. "Staff," "Psychical Research," and "Trees and Plants." The United States government had its say in Arthur J. Ellis, *The Divining Rod: A History of Water-Witching*, Water Supply Paper 416 (1917; reprint Washington, D.C.: Government Printing Office, 1938).

The career of Guy Fenley, The Boy with the X-Ray Eyes, is described in "Some Bold Statements," Alpine (Texas) *Avalanche*, November 30, 1900 (reprinted from the San Antonio *Herald*). Also in the *Avalanche* were two brief follow-ups, both on February 8, 1901. Wigfall Van Sickle's comment on young Fenley is found in Barrett and Besterman, *The Divining Rod*, pp. 196–198, which also lists newspaper articles about the boy.

Mrs. Pat Wedin of Marathon told me about John Hackett, whom she knew, and Perry Cartwright told me about himself. In a letter of March 8, 1976, Bill Gardner told me about witching his well. Shortly afterward I rode about the Sunny Glen waterfield in a pickup listening to the views of Dr. W. E. Lockhart, on my left, and to the experiences of Bob Stevens, on my right.

In a flurry of interest in witching, H. Allen Smith borrowed my notes and in part used John Hackett as the basis for a character in *Return of the Virginian* (New York: Doubleday, 1974).

6.

The Steer Branded MURDER

A detailed and thoroughly researched account of this story is Barry Scobee, *The Steer Branded Murder* (Houston: The Frontier Press, 1952). This contains Robert Powe's eye-witness recollection of the murder of his father, an account of the killing of the culprit Finus Gilliland, biographical information on Manning Clements, and the remarks of lawyer Wigfall Van Sickle and others. Only two details are left unclear by Scobee, one being whether the bull was castrated, the other being the size and location of the brand or brands. There is a brief account in Carlysle Graham Raht, *The Romance of the Davis Mountains and Big Bend Country* (El Paso: The Rahtbooks Co., 1919), pp. 305–306. Virginia Madison adds a few details of the legend in *The Big Bend Country of Texas* (Albuquerque: The University of New Mexico Press, 1955), pp. 145–146. The first name of Finus Gilliland is established in Clifford B. Casey, *Mysteries, Mirages, and Reality: Brewster County Texas of the Big Bend of the Rio Grande* (Hereford, Texas: Pioneer Book Publishers, Inc., 1972), pp. 326–327. I quote Wayland Hand, "Fear of the Gods: Superstition and Popular Belief," in Tristram P. Coffin (ed.), *Our Living Traditions* (New York: Basic Books, 1968), p. 216. Biblical words on the scapegoat are in Lev. 14: 10 and 21; the blood words are in Gen. 4: 10–11.

An intriguing account is that by Mrs. Jack Shipman, "The Lone Red Murder Yearling of West Texas," in *Voice of the Mexican Border* (February–March, 1934), pp. 271–273. In it a long quotation from Van Sickle bears all the earmarks of the article he wrote for a Galveston paper in 1896. He goes on to tell of killings other than that of Henry Powe and seems to be the source of Raht's earlier account. Either Van Sickle had gone over the same ground when interviewed by Mrs. Shipman or both she and Raht had access to the same clipping.

7.
Indian Emily and Dolores

The *ur*-preservers of many a legend of the Big Bend are Carlysle Graham Raht and Barry Scobee. Raht gives us Indian Emily in *The Romance of the Davis Mountains and the Big Bend Country* (El Paso: The Rahtbooks Co., 1919), pp. 171–173. Scobee gives us Indian Emily and Dolores twice, first in his 1947 history of Fort Davis and again in his 1963 revision: *Old Fort Davis* (San Antonio: The Naylor Co., 1947), pp. 41–62, 79–81, with Major Clapp's poem, "Dolores," pp. 81–84, and *Fort Davis Texas, 1583–1960* (San Antonio: The Naylor Co., 1963), pp. 56–57, 124, 206. Virginia Madison tells the tale in *The Big Bend Country of Texas* (Albuquerque: University of New Mexico Press, 1955), pp. 38–39, and Louise Cheney in "Why Indian Em'ly Saved Fort Davis," which comes to me as an undated tearsheet from *The West* magazine. Individual informants are mentioned in the text.

Bruce Lamberson, a Sul Ross State University graduate student in history working with Fort Davis records, provided me with the reference to Mr. Easton (Fort Davis microfilm collection, Roll NMRA 63-146 [1777] RG 98, 1st Lt. W. I. Sanborn . . . to Captain Hunt, Sept. 23, 1871; and Roll NMRA 783 [7675] 8, RG, Letters

Received, Post Adjutant, Thomas Hunt) and to Thomas Nelson (Roll BMRA 66-783 [7675] 6, RG, 98, Records of the U.S. Army Command, Fort Davis, Selected Documents, 1867–1891, "Proceedings of a Board of Officers by Special Orders No. 96, p. 4).

Faye Carr Adams' poem, "Em'ly, the Chieftain's Daughter," comes to me by way of an offprint from her book of poems. The quote is from *Sweet Is the Homing Hour* (Dallas: The Kaleidograph Press, 1948), pp. 77.

8.
John Glanton, Scalp Hunter

One of the earliest tale tellers to dwell at length on John Glanton is Horace Bell in *Reminiscences of a Ranger* (Los Angeles: 1881). Writing long before Bell, Samuel E. Chamberlain was saying in the 1850s that he was a member of Glanton's gang of scalp hunters (*My Confession* [New York: Harper & Bros.; 1956], pp. 39–41 and 255–297.) Glanton's family is outlined in Frederick A. Chabot, *With the Makers of San Antonio* (San Antonio: Artes Graficas, 1937), p. 106.

The yarns about Glanton's taking pot shots at preachers comes from W. W. McCullough of West Chester, Pennsylvania. He wrote a letter to *Life* about it (August 27, 1956; p. 13), and after I wrote to him, he sent me a fuller account in a copy of Ress Phares, "Fabulous Forties Had Murder, Inc.," Dallas *Morning News*, December 30, 1955. With McCullough's letter in *Life* is printed a pictorial representation of John Glanton, as recollected by Sam Chamberlain, author of *My Confession*.

General Zachary Taylor's disgusted estimate of the Texas Rangers is quoted in Stanley Vestal, *Big Foot Wallace: A Biography* (Boston: Houghton Mifflin Co., 1942), p. 236. The general's wrath at Glanton's uncivilized warfaring is described by Walter P. Lane in *Adventures and Recollections of General Walter P. Lane, A San Jacinto Veteran* (Marshall, Texas: News-Messenger Publishing Co., 1928), pp. 55–59. I have transformed some of the indirect quotations in this source and others into dialogue.

Glanton's deal with the Chihuahua government is found in the *Texas State Gazette*, September 1, 7, and October 7, 1849. A bit more detail about the bounties offered by Chihuahua and Sonora is found in Hubert Howe Bancroft, *History of Mexico* (San Francisco: A. L. Bancroft & Co., 1885), 5: 579 and 597 n.

Correspondence of Chihuahua Governor Angel Trias, Major

General George M. Brooke, and Major Jefferson Van Horne concerning John Glanton is reproduced by Mabel Lowry in "Fort Leaton State Historical Park, Presidio County, Texas," the report she prepared for the Park Services Division, Texas Parks and Wildlife Department, Austin, Texas, 1969.

The Glanton raid near Santa Helena Canyon is described in Colonel Richard Irving Dodge, *Our Wild Indians*, (Hartford, Connecticut: A. D. Worthington & Co., 1883), p. 245. Julius Froebel's *Seven Years Travel Through Central America* (1859) is quoted by Leavitt Corning, Jr., in *Baronial Forts of the Big Bend* (San Antonio: Trinity University Press, 1967), p. 29.

Jack Hays' unsuccessful plea to Glanton to let the Apaches alone is recounted in Bertha Blount, "The Apaches in the Southwest, 1846–1886," *Southwestern Historical Quarterly*, 23 (July, 1919): 20–21. An account of Indian hater Jeff Turner is told by John C. Duval in *The Adventures of Big Foot Wallace*, ed. Mable Major and Rebecca W. Smith (Lincoln: University of Nebraska Press, 1966), chapters 17–19, and Herman Melville tells about his Indian hater, Colonel John Moredock, in *The Confidence Man*, chapters 25–28.

One version of the Yuma conquest of Glanton at Fort Defiance is that in John Russell Bartlett, *Personal Narrative of Explorations and Incidents in Texas, New Mexico, California, Sonora, and Chihuahua, Connected with the United States and Mexican Boundary Commission During the Years 1850, '51, and '53* (New York: D. Appleton & Co., 1854), 2: 174–175.

The roster of ten members of the gang killed at Yuma Crossing is contained in Grant Foreman, *Marcy and the Gold Seekers* (Norman: University of Oklahoma Press, 1939), p. 336, as taken from a newspaper account of the event. Besides John Glanton, Texan, they are:

Dr. A. L. Lincoln, St. Louis	Henderson Smith, Missouri
John Hackson, New York	John Gunn, Missouri
William Pewit, Texas	Thomas Wilson, Philadelphia
John Dorsey, Missouri	James M. Miller, New Jersey
Thomas Harlan, Texas	John Jackson, a Negro

Other members of the gang, named by Samuel E. Chamberlain, are:

Crying Tom Hitchcock	Ben Tobin
Judge Holden	Doc Irving
Mountain Jim	Dick Shelby
Long Webster	Sam Tate
Charley McIntosh, a Cherokee	

Named by Horace Bell are:
  Charley Brown
  Dave Brown
Chamberlain's editor, Roger Butterfield, discovered three names
signed in Los Angeles to a deposition describing the massacre which
they escaped:
  Joseph A. Anderson
  William Carr
  Marcus L. Webster
It is probable that many if not all of these names are aliases, except
for those of Samuel E. Chamberlain and Marcus Long Webster.

9.
Bobcat Carter

The chief source for this chapter is the paper by C. Ross
Burns, "Bobcat Carter, Hermit of the Big Bend," prepared in 1972
when he was a student at Sul Ross State University, working under
a David Witts Folklore Studies Grant. Burns' sources in turn con-
sisted partly of the William A. Cooper, Jr., collection in Snyder,
Texas, of such papers and snapshots Carter left behind in his tin
shed when he died. These include the passport issued to Carter in
Acuña, Mexico, which attests to the place and date of Carter's birth.
Burns' other sources include many interviews with people who
knew Carter or had heard about him. Burns also located the cer-
tificate of death of Henry Carter at the Brewster county clerk's
office. I have referred also to Virginia Madison, *The Big Bend Country of Texas* (Albuquerque: University of New Mexico Press,
1955), p. 5, and to "The Border Trading Posts" in W. D. Smithers,
*Nature's Pharmacy and the Curanderos; And, The Border Trading
Posts*, Publications of the West Texas Historical and Scientific
Society no. 18, Sul Ross State College Bulletin, vol. 41, no. 3 (September 1, 1961), pp. 41–55.

In *Return of the Virginian* (New York: Doubleday, 1974),
H. Allen Smith based his former lightning rod salesman in part on
Bobcat Carter.

10.
The Lost Haystack Mine

For stories about this lost mine, I am indebted to my good friends
named in the article, Barton Warnock, Art Gard, Bill Lane, Buddy
Lane, Joe Brady, Walter Vick, Harold Page, and Mary Ella Vannoy.

11.

The Marfa Lights

Ferdinand Weber saw the lights in 1927 and told Riley Aiken about it for "More Chisos Ghosts," in Mody C. Boatright et al. (eds.), *Madstones and Twisters,* Publications of the Texas Folklore Society no. 28 (Dallas: Southern Methodist University Press, 1958), pp. 123–127. The 1883 and prior sightings are told by Marge Crumbaker in "The Unsolved Mystery of the Ghost Lights," in *Texas Tempo,* Sunday magazine in the Houston *Post,* January 7, 1968, copies of which are given away by the Alpine Chamber of Commerce. Mrs. Hallie Stillwell, Alpine justice of the peace, is quoted in Harry Wood, "Indian Ghost Light," San Angelo *Standard-Times,* January 14, 1965, p. B–1.

Folklorist Joe Graham lent me his collection of Marfa Lights stories collected and written up by his well-guided students. There are also several I collected myself that went into sorting out and arranging the main lines of legendry that go with the Marfa Lights. Individual informants are mentioned in the text.

Similiar mystery lights in other parts of the country were described in a *Saga* magazine article published in 1971. It named the lights near Sarasota, Texas, eleven others in the United States, and one each in South America and Canada.

12.

More Recent Sources

Chapter 5: Frank Tolbert, "The X-ray Eyes," Dallas *Morning News,* February 24, 1979, p. 3D. At 79 Guy Fenley said: "They claimed I could see right through the ground. I couldn't. What I had was a kind of feeling, an inner vision." Fenley lost his "gift" by age twenty-three, he said, because his family used it to make money. "That's what it was, a gift. A gift to help other people."

Chapter 8: See Louise K. Barnett, *Nineteenth Century Indian Hater Fiction* (Durham, N.C.: Duke University Press, 1975).

Index

CPSIA information can be obtained at www.ICGtesting.com
Printed in the USA
LVOW062226050912

297583LV00001B/5/P